Medieval English Literature

Neil Gunnister
May 1970.

W. P. KER

Medieval English Literature

OXFORD UNIVERSITY PRESS
London Oxford New York

Oxford University Press

OXFORD LONDON NEW YORK

GLASGOW TORONTO MELBOURNE WELLINGTON

CAPE TOWN SALISBURY IBADAN NAIROBI LUSAKA ADDIS ABABA

BOMBAY CALCUTTA MADRAS KARACHI LAHORE DACCA

KUALA LUMPUR SINGAPORE HONG KONG TOKYO

First published in the Home University Library 1912
First issued as an Oxford University Press paperback 1969

PRINTED IN GREAT BRITAIN

Contents

1
Introduction

READERS ARE DRAWN to medieval literature in many different ways, and it is hardly possible to describe all the attractions and all the approaches by which they enter on this ground. Students of history have to learn the languages of the nations with whose history they are concerned, and to read the chief books in those languages, if they wish to understand rightly the ideas, purposes and temper of the past ages. Sometimes the study of early literature has been instigated by religious or controversial motives, as when the Anglo-Saxon homilies were taken up and edited and interpreted in support of the Reformation. Sometimes it is mere curiosity that leads to investigation of old literature—a wish to find out the meaning of what looks at first difficult and mysterious. Curiosity of this sort, however, is seldom found unmixed; there are generally all sorts of vague associations and interests combining to lead the explorer on. It has often been observed that a love of Gothic architecture, or medieval art in general, goes along with, and helps, the study of medieval poetry. Chatterton's old English reading and his imitations of old English verse were inspired by the Church of St. Mary Redcliffe at Bristol. The lives of Horace Walpole, of Thomas Warton, of Sir Walter Scott, and many others show how medieval literary studies may be nourished along with other kindred antiquarian tastes.

Sometimes, instead of beginning in historical or antiquarian interests, or in a liking for the fashions of the Middle Ages in general, it happens that a love of medieval literature has its rise in one particular author, e.g. Dante or Sir Thomas Malory. The book, the *Divina Commedia* or *Le Morte d'Arthur*, is taken up, it may be, casually, with no very distinct idea or purpose, and then it is found to be engrossing and captivating—what is often rightly called 'a revelation of a new world'. For a long time this is enough in itself; the reader is content with Dante or with the *Morte d'Arthur*. But it may occur to him to ask about 'the French book' from which Malory got his adventures of the Knights of King Arthur; he may want to know how the legend of the Grail came to be mixed up with the romances of the Round Table; and so he will be drawn on, trying to find out as much as possible and plunging deeper and deeper into the Middle Ages. The same kind of thing happens to the reader of Dante; Dante is found all through his poem acknowledging obliga-tions of earlier writers; he is not alone or independent in his thought and his poetry; and so it becomes an interesting thing to go further back and to know something about the older poets and moralists, and the earlier medieval world in general, before it was all summed up and recorded in the imagination of the Divine Comedy. Examples of this way of reading may be found in the works of Ruskin and in Matthew Arnold. Matthew Arnold, rather late in his life (in the introductory essay to T. H. Ward's *English Poets*), shows that he has been reading some old French authors. He does not begin with old French when he is young; evidently he was brought to it in working back from the better known poets, Dante and Chaucer. Ruskin's old French quotations are also rather late in the series of his writings; it was in his Oxford lectures, partly published in *Fors Clavigera*, that he dealt with *The Romance of the Rose,* and used it to illustrate whatever else was in his mind at the time.

   Thus it is obvious that any one who sets out to write about English literature in the Middle Ages will find himself addressing an audi-ence which is not at all in agreement with regard to the subject. Some will probably be historical in their tastes, and will seek, in literature, for information about manners and customs, fashions of opinion, 'typical developments' in the history of culture or education. Others may be on the look-out for stories, for the charm of romance which is sometimes thought to belong peculiarly to the Middle Ages, and some, with ambitions of their own, may ask for themes that can be used and adapted in modern forms, as the Nibelung story has been used by Wagner and William Morris and many others; perhaps for mere suggestions of plots and scenery, to be employed more freely, as in Morris's prose romances, for example. Others, starting from one favourite author—Dante or Chaucer or Malory—will try to place what they already know in its right relation to all its surroundings—by working, for instance, at the history of religious poetry, or the different kinds of story-telling. It is not easy to write for all these and for other different tastes as well. But it is not a hopeless business, so long as there is some sort of interest to begin with, even if it be only a general vague curiosity about an unknown subject.

There are many prejudices against the Middle Ages; the name itself was originally an expression of contempt; it means the interval of darkness between the ruin of ancient classical culture and the modern revival of learning—a time supposed to be full of ignorance, superstition and bad taste, an object of loathing to well-educated persons. As an example of this sort of opinion about the Middle Ages, one may take what Bentham says of our 'barbarian ancestors' —'few of whom could so much as read, and those few had nothing before them that was worth the reading'. 'When from their ordinary occupation, their order of the day, the cutting of one another's throats, or those of Welshmen, Scotchmen or Irishmen, they could steal now and then a holiday, how did they employ it? In cutting Frenchmen's throats in order to get their money: this was active virtue:—leaving Frenchmen's throats uncut was indolence, slumber, inglorious ease.'

On the other hand, the Middle Ages have been glorified by many writers; 'the Age of Chivalry', the 'Ages of Faith' have often been contrasted with the hardness of the age of enlightenment, rationalism, and material progress; they are thought of as full of colour, variety, romance of all sorts, while modern civilization is represented as comparatively dull, monotonous and unpicturesque. This kind of view has so far prevailed, even among people who do not go to any extremes, and who are not excessively enthusiastic or romantic, that the term 'Gothic', which used to be a term of contempt for the Middle Ages, has entirely lost its scornful associations. 'Gothic' was originally an abusive name, like 'Vandalism'; it meant the same thing as 'barbarian'. But while 'Vandalism' has kept its bad meaning, 'Gothic' has lost it. It does not now mean 'barbarous', and if it still means 'unclassical' it does not imply that what is 'unclassical' must be wrong. It is possible now to think of the Middle Ages and their literature without prejudice on the one side or the other. As no one now thinks of despising Gothic architecture simply because it is not Greek, so the books of the Middle Ages may be read in a spirit of fairness by those who will take the trouble to understand their language; they may be appreciated for what they really are; their goodness or badness is not now determined merely by comparison with the work of other times in which the standards and ideals of excellence were not the same.

The language is a difficulty. The older English books are written in the language which is commonly called Anglo-Saxon; this is certainly not one of the most difficult, but no language is really easy to learn. Anglo-Saxon poetry, besides, has a peculiar vocabulary and strange forms of expression. The poetical books are not to be read without a great deal of application; they cannot be rushed.

Later, when the language has changed into what is technically called Middle English—say, in the thirteenth century—things are in many ways no better. It is true that the language is nearer to modern English; it is true also that the language of the poetical books is generally much simpler and nearer that of ordinary prose than was the language of the Anglo-Saxon poets. But on the other hand, while Anglo-Saxon literature is practically all in one language, Middle English is really not a language at all, but a great number of different tongues, belonging to different parts of the country. And not only does the language of Yorkshire differ from that of Kent, or Dorset, or London, or Lancashire, but within the same district each author spells as he pleases, and the man who makes a copy of his book also spells as he pleases, and mixes up his own local and personal varieties with those of the original author. There is besides an enormously greater amount of written matter extant in Middle English than in Anglo-Saxon, and this, coming from all parts of the country, is full of all varieties of odd words. The vocabulary of Middle English, with its many French and Danish words, its many words belonging to one region and not to another, is, in some ways, more difficult than that of Anglo-Saxon.

But luckily it is not hard, in spite of all these hindrances, to make a fair beginning with the old languages—in Anglo-Saxon, for example, with Sweet's *Primer* and *Reader*, in Middle English with Chaucer or *Piers Plowman*.

The difference in language between Anglo-Saxon and Middle English corresponds to a division in the history of literature. Anglo-Saxon literature is different from that which follows it, not merely in its grammar and dictionary, but in many of its ideas and fashions, particularly in its fashion of poetry. The difference may be expressed in this way, that while the older English literature is mainly English, the literature after the eleventh century is largely dependent on France; France from 1100 to 1400 is the chief source of ideas, culture, imagination, stories, and forms of verse. It is sometimes thought that this was the result of the Norman Conquest, but this is not the proper explanation of what happened, either in language or in literature. For the same kind of thing happened in other countries which were not conquered by the Normans or by any other people speaking French. The history of the German language and of German literature in the Middle Ages corresponds in many things to the history of English. The name Middle English was invented by a German Philologist (Grimm), who found in English the same stages of development as in German; Anglo-Saxon corresponds to Old German in its inflexions; Middle English is like Middle German. The change, in both languages, is a change from one kind of inflexion to another. In the 'Old' stage (say, about the year 900) the inflexions have various clearly pronounced vowels in them; in the 'Middle' stage (about 1200) the terminations of words have come to be pronounced less distinctly, and where there is inflexion it shows most commonly one vowel, written *e*, when the 'Old' form might have *a* or *o* or *u*. Changes of this kind had begun in England before the Norman Conquest, and would have gone on as they did in Germany if there had been no Norman Conquest at all. The French and the French language had nothing to do with it.

Where the French were really important was in their ideas and in the forms of their poetry; they made their influence felt through these in all Western Christendom, in Italy, in Denmark, and even more strongly in Germany than in England. Indeed it might be said that the Norman Conquest made it less easy for the English than it was for the Germans to employ the French ideas when they were writing books of their own in their own language. The French influence was too strong in England; the native language was discouraged; many Englishmen wrote their books in French, instead of making English adaptations from the French. The Germans, who were independent politically, were not tempted in the same way as the English, and in many respects they were more successful than the English as translators from the French, as adapters of French 'motives' and ideas. But whatever the differences might be between one nation and another, it is certain that after 1100 French ideas were appreciated in all the countries of Europe, in such a way as to make France the principal source of enlightenment and entertainment everywhere; and the intellectual predominance of France is what most of all distinguishes the later medieval from the earlier, that is, from the Anglo-Saxon period, in the history of English literature.

The leadership of France in the literature of Europe may be dated as beginning about 1100, which is the time of the First Crusade and of many great changes in the life of Christendom. About 1100 there is an end of one great historical period, which began with what is called the Wandering of the German Nations, and their settlement in various parts of the world. The Norman Conquest of England, it has been said, is the last of the movements in the wandering of the nations. Goths and Vandals, Franks, Burgundians, Lombards, Angles, Jutes and Saxons, Danes and Northmen, had all had their times of adventure, exploration, conquest and settlement. One great event in this wandering was the establishment of the Norwegian settlers in France, the foundation of Normandy; and the expeditions of the Normans—to Italy as well as to England—were nearly the last which were conducted in the old style. After the Norman Conquest there are new sorts of adventure, which are represented in Chaucer's Knight and Squire—the one a Crusader, or Knight errant, the other (his son) engaged in a more modern sort of warfare, England against France, nation against nation.

INTRODUCTION 13

The two forms of the English language, Anglo-Saxon and Middle English, and the two periods of medieval English literature, correspond to the two historical periods of which one ends and the other begins about 1100, at the date of the First Crusade. Anglo-Saxon literature belongs to the older world; Anglo-Saxon poetry goes back to very early times and keeps a tradition which had come down from ancient days when the English were still a Continental German tribe. Middle English literature is cut off from Anglo-Saxon, the Anglo-Saxon stories are forgotten, and though the old alliterative verse is kept, as late as the sixteenth century, it is in a new form with a new tune in it; while instead of being the one great instrument of poetry it has to compete with rhyming couplets and stanzas of different measure; it is hard put to it by the rhymes of France.

2

The Anglo-Saxon Period

IN DEALING WITH Anglo-Saxon literature it is well to remember
first of all that comparatively little of it has been preserved; we cannot be sure, either, that the best things have been preserved, in the
poetry especially. Anglo-Saxon poetry was being made, we know, for
at least five hundred years. What now exists is found, chiefly, in
four manuscript volumes,[1] which have been saved, more or less accidentally, from all sorts of dangers. No one can say what has been
lost. Many manuscripts, as good as any of these, may have been sold
as old parchment, or given to the children to cut up into tails for
kites. One Anglo-Saxon poem, *Waldere*, is known from two fragments of it which were discovered in the binding of a book in
Copenhagen. Two other poems were fortunately copied and published about two hundred years ago by two famous antiquaries; the
original manuscripts have disappeared since then. Who can tell how
many manuscripts have disappeared without being copied? The
obvious conclusion is that we can speak about what we know, but
not as if we knew everything about Anglo-Saxon poetry.

With the prose it is rather different. The prose translations due to
King Alfred are preserved; so is the English Chronicle; so are a fair
number of religious works, the homilies of Ælfric and others; it does
not seem likely from what we know of the conditions of authorship

[1] The Cædmon MS. in Oxford.
The Exeter Book.
The Vercelli Book.
The book containing the poems *Beowulf* and *Judith* in the Cotton Library at
the British Museum.

in those times that any prose work of any notable or original value has disappeared. With the poetry, on the other hand, every fresh discovery—like that of the bookbinding fragments already mentioned—makes one feel that the extent of Anglo-Saxon poetry is unknown. Anything may turn up. We cannot say what subjects were not treated by Anglo-Saxon poets. It is certain that many good stories were known to them which are not found in any of the extant manuscripts.

The contents of Anglo-Saxon literature may be divided into two sections, one belonging to the English as a Teutonic people who inherited along with their language a form of poetry and a number of stories which have nothing to do with Roman civilization; the other derived from Latin and turning into English the knowledge which was common to the whole of Europe.

The English in the beginning—Angles and Saxons—were heathen Germans who took part in the great movement called the Wandering of the Nations—who left their homes and emigrated to lands belonging to the Roman empire, and made slaves of the people they found there. They were barbarians; the civilized inhabitants of Britain, when the English appeared there, thought of them as horrible savages. They were as bad and detestable as the Red Indians were to the Colonists in America long afterwards.

But we know that the early English are not to be judged entirely by the popular opinion of the Britons whom they harried and enslaved, any more than the English of Queen Elizabeth's time are to be thought of simply according to the Spanish ideas about Sir Francis Drake. There were centuries of an old civilization behind them when they settled in Britain; what it was like is shown partially in the work of the Bronze and the early Iron Age in the countries from which the English came. The *Germania* of Tacitus tells more, and more still is to be learned from the remains of the old poetry.

Tacitus was not quite impartial in his account of the Germans; he used them as examples to point a moral against the vices of Rome; the German, in his account, is something like the 'noble savage' who was idealized by later philosophers in order to chastise the faults of sophisticated modern life. But Tacitus, though he might have been rather inclined to favour the Germans, was mainly a scientific observer who wished to find out the truth about them, and to write a clear description of their manners and customs. One of the proofs of his success is the agreement between his *Germania* and the pictures of life composed by the people of that race themselves in their epic poetry.

The case of the early English is very like that of the Danes and Northmen four or five hundred years later. The Anglo-Saxons thought and wrote of the Danes almost exactly as the Britons had thought of their Saxon enemies. The English had to suffer from the Danish pirates what the Britons had suffered from the English; they cursed the Danes as their own ancestors had been cursed by the Britons; the invaders were utterly detestable and fiendish men of blood. But luckily we have some other information about those pirates. From the Norwegian, Danish and Icelandic historians, and from some parts of the old Northern poetry, there may be formed a different idea about the character and domestic manners of the men who made themselves so unpleasant in their visits to the English and the neighbouring coasts. The pirates at home were peaceful country gentlemen, leading respectable and beneficent lives among their poorer neighbours. The Icelandic histories—including the history of Norway for three or four centuries—may be consulted for the domestic life of the people who made so bad a name for themselves as plunderers abroad. They appear there, several varieties of them, as members of a reasonable, honourable community, which could have given many lessons of civilization to England or France many centuries later. But the strangest and most convincing evidence about the domestic manners of the Northmen is found in English, and is written by King Alfred himself. King Alfred had many foreigners in his service, and one of them was a Norwegian gentleman from the far North, named Ohthere (or Ottárr, as it would be in the Norse tongue rather later than King Alfred's time). How he came into the King's service is not known, but there are other accounts of similar cases which show how easy it was for Northmen of ability to make their way in the world through the patronage of kings. Ohthere belonged exactly to the class from which the most daring and successful rovers came. He was a gentleman of good position at home in Halogaland (now called Helgeland in the north of Norway), a landowner with various interests, attending to his crops, making a good deal out of trade with the Finns and Lapps; and besides that a navigator, the first who rounded the North Cape and sailed into the White Sea. His narrative, which is given by Alfred as an addition to his translation of Orosius, makes a pleasant and amusing contrast to the history of the Danish wars, which also may have been partly written by King Alfred himself for their proper place in the English Chronicle.

As the Icelandic sagas and Ohthere's narrative and other documents make it easy to correct the prejudiced and partial opinions of the English about the Danes, so the opinions of the Britons about the Saxons are corrected, though the evidence is not by any means so clear. The Angles and Saxons, like the Danes and Northmen later—like Sir Francis Drake, or like Ulysses, we might say—were occasionally pirates, but not restricted to that profession. They had many other things to do and think about. Before everything, they belonged to the great national system which Tacitus calls *Germania*—which was never politically united, even in the loosest way, but which nevertheless was a unity, conscious of its separation from all the foreigners whom it called, in a comprehensive manner, Welsh. In England the Welsh are the Cambro-Britons; in Germany Welsh means sometimes French, sometimes Italian—a meaning preserved in the name 'walnut' (or 'walsh-note', as it is in Chaucer)—the 'Italian nut'. Those who are not Welsh are 'Teutonic'—which is not a mere modern pedantic name, but is used by old writers in the same way as by modern philologists, and applied to High or Low Dutch indifferently, and also to English. But the unity of *Germania* —the community of sentiment among the early German nations— does not need to be proved by such philological notes as the opposition of 'Dutch' and 'Welsh'. It is proved by its own most valuable results, by its own 'poetical works'—the heroic legends which were held in common by all the nations of *Germania*. If any one were to ask, 'What does the old English literature *prove*?' the answer would be ready enough. It proves that the Germanic nations had a reciprocal free trade in subjects for epic poems. They were generally free from local jealousy about heroes. Instead of a natural rivalry among Goths, Burgundians and the rest, the early poets seem to

have had a liking for heroes not of their own nation, so long as
they were members of one of the German tribes. (The Huns, it may
be here remarked, are counted as Germans; Attila is not thought of
as a barbarian.) The great example of this common right in heroes
is Sigfred, Sigurd the Volsung, Siegfried of the *Nibelungenlied*. His
original stock and race is of no particular interest to any one; he is a
hero everywhere, and everywhere he is thought of as belonging, in
some way or other, to the people who sing about him. This glory of
Sigurd or Siegfried is different from the later popularity of King
Arthur or of Charlemagne in countries outside of Britain or
France. Arthur and Charlemagne are adopted in many places as
favourite heroes without any particular thought of their nationality,
in much the same way as Alexander the Great was celebrated everywhere from pure love of adventurous stories. But Siegfried or
Sigurd, whether in High or Low Germany, or Norway, or Iceland, is always at home. He is not indeed a national champion,
like the Cid in Spain or the Wallace in Scotland, but everywhere
he is thought of, apart from any local attachment, as the hero of
the race.

One of the old English poems called *Widsith* (the Far Traveller)
is an epitome of the heroic poetry of *Germania*, and a clear proof of
the common interest taken in all the heroes. The theme of the poem
·is the wandering of a poet, who makes his way to the courts of the
most famous kings: Ermanaric the Goth, Gundahari the Burgun-
dian, Alboin the Lombard, and many more. The poem is a kind of
fantasia, intended to call up, by allusion, the personages of the most
famous stories; it is not an epic poem, but it plays with some of the
plots of heroic poetry familiar throughout the whole Teutonic
region. Ermanaric and Gundahari, here called Eormanric and
Guthhere, are renowned in the old Scandinavian poetry, and the old
High German. Guthhere is one of the personages in the poem of
Waldere; what is Guthhere in English is Gunnar in Norse, Gunther
in German—the Gunther of the *Nibelungenlied*. Offa comes into
Widsith's record, an English king; but he has no particular mark or
eminence or attraction to distinguish him in the poet's favour from
the Goth or the Lombard; he is king of 'Ongle', the original Anglia
to the south of Jutland, and there is no room for doubt that the

English when they lived there and when they invaded Britain had the stories of all the Teutonic heroes at their command to occupy their minds, if they chose to listen to the lay of the minstrel. What they got from their minstrels was a number of stories about all the famous men of the Teutonic race—stories chanted in rhythmical verse and noble diction, presenting tragic themes and pointing the moral of heroism.

Of this old poetry there remains one work nearly complete. *Beowulf*, because it is extant, has sometimes been over-valued, as if it were the work of an English Homer. But it was not preserved as the *Iliad* was, by the unanimous judgement of all the people through successive generations. It must have been of some importance at one time, or it would not have been copied out fair as a handsome book for the library of some gentleman. But many trashy things have been equally honoured in gentlemen's libraries, and it cannot be shown that *Beowulf* was nearly the best of its class. It was preserved by an accident; it has no right to the place of the most illustrious Anglo-Saxon epic poem. The story is commonplace and the plan is feeble. But there are some qualities in it which make it (accidentally or not, it hardly matters) the best worth studying of all the Anglo-Saxon poems. It is the largest extant piece in any old Teutonic language dealing poetically with native Teutonic subjects. It is the largest and fullest picture of life in the order to which it belongs; the only thing that shows incontestably the power of the old heroic poetry to deal on a fairly large scale with subjects taken from the national tradition. The impression left by *Beowulf*, when the carping critic has done his worst, is that of a noble manner of life, of courtesy and freedom, with the dignity of tragedy attending it, even though the poet fails, or does not attempt, to work out fully any proper tragic theme of his own.

There is a very curious likeness in many details between *Beowulf* and the *Odyssey*; but quite apart from the details there is a real likeness between them in their 'criticism of life'—i.e. in their exhibition of human motives and their implied or expressed opinions about human conduct. There is the same likeness between the *Odyssey* and the best of the Icelandic Sagas—particularly the *Story of Burnt Njal*; and the lasting virtue of *Beowulf* is that it is bred in the same sort of world as theirs. It is not so much the valour and devotion of the hero; it is the conversation of the hosts and guests in the King's hall, the play of serious and gentle moods in the minds of the freeborn, that gives its character to the poem. *Beowulf,* through its rendering of noble manners, its picture of good society, adds something distinct and unforgettable to the records of the past. There is life in it, and a sort of life which would be impossible without centuries of training, of what Spenser called 'vertuous and gentle discipline'.

Beowulf is worth studying, among other reasons, because it brings out one great difference between the earlier and later medieval poetry, between Anglo-Saxon and Middle English taste in fiction. *Beowulf* is a tale of adventure; the incidents in it are such as may be found in hundreds of other stories. Beowulf himself, the hero, is a champion and a slayer of monsters. He hears that the King of the Danes is plagued in his house by the visits of an ogre, who night after night comes and carries off one of the King's men. He goes on a visit to Denmark, sits up for the ogre, fights with him and mortally wounds him. That does not end the business, for the ogre's mother comes to revenge her son, and Beowulf has a second fight and kills her too, and is thanked and goes home again. Many years afterwards when he is king in his own country, Gautland (which is part of modern Sweden), a fiery dragon is accidentally stirred up from a long sleep and makes itself a pest in the country. Beowulf goes to attack the dragon, fights and wins, but is himself killed by the poison of the dragon. The poem ends with his funeral. So told, in abstract, it is not a particularly interesting story. Told in the same bald way, the story of Theseus or of Hercules would still have much more in it; there are many more adventures than this in later romances like *Sir Bevis of Southampton* or *Sir Huon of Bordeaux.* What makes the poem of *Beowulf* really interesting, and different from the later romances, is that it is full of all sorts of references and allusions to great events, to the fortunes of kings and nations, which seem to come in naturally, as if the author had in his mind the whole history of all the people who were in any way connected with Beowulf, and could not keep his knowledge from showing itself. There is an historical background. In romances, and also in popular tales, you may get the same sort of adventures as in *Beowulf*, but they are told in quite a different way. They have nothing to do with reality. In *Beowulf*, the historical allusions are so many, and given with such a conviction of their importance and their truth, that they draw away the attention from the main events of the story—the fights with the ogre Grendel and his mother, and the killing of the dragon. This is one of the faults of the poem. The story is rather thin and poor. But in another way those distracting allusions to things apart from the chief story make up for their want of proportion. They give the impression of reality and weight; the story is not in the air, or in a fabulous country like that of Spenser's *Faerie Queene*; it is part of the solid world. It would be difficult to find anything like this in later medieval romance. It is this, chiefly, that makes *Beowulf* a true *epic* poem—that is, a narrative poem of the most stately and serious kind.

The history in it is not English history; the personages in it are Danes, Gauts, and Swedes. One of them, Hygelac, the king whom Beowulf succeeded, is identified with a king named by the Frankish historian Gregory of Tours; the date is about A.D. 515. The epic poem of *Beowulf* has its source pretty far back, in the history of countries not very closely related to England. Yet the English hearers of the poem were expected to follow the allusions, and to be interested in the names and histories of Swedish, Gautish, and Danish kings. As if that was not enough, there is a story within the story—a poem of adventure is chanted by a minstrel at the Danish Court, and the scene of this poem is in Friesland. There is no doubt that it was a favourite subject, for the Frisian story is mentioned in the poem of Widsith, the Traveller; and more than that, there is an independent version of it among the few remains of Anglo-Saxon heroic poetry—*The Fight at Finnesburh*. Those who listened to heroic songs in England seem to have had no peculiar liking for English subjects. Their heroes belong to *Germania*. The same thing is found in Norway and Iceland, where the favourite hero is Sigurd. His story, the story of the Volsungs and Niblungs, comes from Germany. In *Beowulf* there is a reference to it—not to Sigfred himself, but to his father Sigemund. Everywhere and in every possible way the old heroic poets seem to escape from the particular nation to which they belong, and to look for their subjects in some other part of the Teutonic system. In some cases, doubtless, this might be due to the same kind of romantic taste as led later authors to place their stories in Greece, or Babylon, or anywhere far from home. But it can scarcely have been so with *Beowulf*; for the author of *Beowulf* does not try to get away from reality; on the contrary, he buttresses his story all round with historical tradition and references to historical fact; he will not let it go forth as pure romance.

The solid foundation and epic weight of *Beowulf* are not exceptional among the Anglo-Saxon poems. There are not many other poems extant of the same class, but there is enough to show that *Beowulf* is not alone. It is a representative work; there were others of the same type; and it is this order of epic poetry which makes the great literary distinction of the Anglo-Saxon period.

It is always necessary to remember how little we know of Anglo-Saxon poetry and generally of the ideas and imaginations of the early English. The gravity and dignity of most of their poetical works are unquestionable; but one ought not to suppose that we know all the varieties of their poetical taste.

It is probable that in the earlier Middle Ages, and in the Teutonic countries, there was a good deal of the fanciful and also of the comic literature which is so frequent in the later Middle Ages (after 1100) and especially in France. One proof of this, for the fanciful and romantic sort of story-telling, will be found in the earlier part of the Danish history written by Saxo Grammaticus. He collected an immense number of stories from Danes and Icelanders—one of them being the story of Hamlet—and although he was comparatively late (writing at the end of the twelfth century), still we know that his stories belong to the North and are unaffected by anything French; they form a body of Northern romance, independent of the French fashions, of King Arthur and Charlemagne. The English historians —William of Malmesbury, e.g.—have collected many things of the same sort. As for comic stories, there are one or two in careful Latin verse, composed in Germany in the tenth century, which show that the same kind of jests were current then as in the later comic poetry of France, in the *Decameron* of Boccaccio, and in the *Canterbury Tales*. The earlier Middle Ages were more like the later Middle Ages than one would think, judging merely from the extant literature of the Anglo-Saxon period on the one hand and the Plantagenet times on the other. But the differences are there, and one of the greatest is between the Anglo-Saxon fashion of epic poetry and the popular romances of the time of Edward I or Edward III.

The difference is brought out in many ways. There is a different choice of subject; the earlier poetry, by preference, is concentrated on one great battle or combat—generally in a place where there is little or no chance of escape—inside a hall, as in *The Fight at Finnesburh*, and in the slaughter 'grim and great' at the end of the *Nibelungenlied*; or, it may be, in a narrow place among rocks, as in the story of Walter of Aquitaine, which is the old English *Waldere*. This is the favourite sort of subject, and it is so because the poets were able thus to hit their audience again and again with increasing force; the effect they aimed at was a crushing impression of strife and danger, and courage growing as the danger grew and the strength lessened. In *Beowulf* the subjects are different, but in *Beowulf* a subject of this sort is introduced, by way of interlude, in the minstrel's song of *Finnesburh*; and also *Beowulf*, with a rather inferior plot, still manages to give the effect and to bring out the spirit of deliberate heroic valour.

Quite late in the Anglo-Saxon period—about the year 1000—there is a poem on an English subject in which this heroic spirit is most thoroughly displayed: the poem on the Battle of Maldon which was fought on the Essex shore in 993 between Byrhtnoth, alderman of East Anglia, and a host of vikings whose leader (though he is not mentioned in the poem) is known as Olaf Tryggvason. By the end of the tenth century Anglo-Saxon poetry had begun to decay. Yet the Maldon poem shows that it was not only still alive, but that in some respects it had made very remarkable progress. There are few examples anywhere of poetry which can deal in a satisfactory way with contemporary heroes. In the Maldon poem, very shortly after the battle, the facts are turned into poetry—into poetry which keeps the form of the older epic, and which in the old manner works up a stronger and stronger swell of courage against the overwhelming ruin. The last word of the heroic age is spoken, five hundred years after the death of Hygelac (above, p. 21), by the old warrior who, like the trusty companion of Beowulf, refused to turn and run when his lord was cut down in the battle:

> Thought shall be the harder, heart the keener,
> Mood the more, as our might lessens.

It is one of the strange things in the history of poetry that in another five hundred years an old fashion of poetry, near akin to the Anglo-Saxon, comes to an end in a poem on a contemporary battle. The last poem in the Middle English alliterative verse, which was used for so many subjects in the fourteenth century—for the stories of Arthur and Alexander and Troy, and for the Vision of Piers Plowman—is the poem of *Scottish Field* A.D. 1513, on the battle of Flodden.

This alliterative verse, which has a history of more than a thousand years, is one of the things that are carried over in some mysterious way from the Anglo-Saxon to the later medieval period. But though it survives the great change in the language, it has a different sound in the fourteenth century from what it has in *Beowulf*; the older verse has a manner of its own.

The Anglo-Saxon poetical forms are difficult at first to understand. The principal rule of the verse is indeed easy enough; it is the same as in the verse of *Piers Plowman*; there is a long line divided in the middle; in each line there are *four* strong syllables; the first *three* of these are generally made alliterative; i.e. they begin with the same consonant—

> Wæs se grimma gæst Grendel haten
> mære mearcstapa, se the móras heold
> fen and fæsten.

> Was the grievous guest Grendel namèd
> mighty mark-stalker, and the moors his home
> fen and fastness.

or they all begin with *different* vowels—

> Eotenas and ylfe and orcneas.

> Etins and elves and ogres too.

But there is a variety and subtilty in the Anglo-Saxon measure which is not found in the Middle English, and which is much more definitely under metrical rules. And apart from the metre of the single line, there is in the older alliterative poetry a skill in composing long passages, best described in the terms which Milton used about his own blank verse: 'the sense variously drawn out from one line to another'. The Anglo-Saxon poets, at their best, are eloquent, and able to carry on for long periods without monotony. Their verse does not fall into detached and separate lines. This habit is another evidence of long culture; Anglo-Saxon poetry, such as we know it, is at the end of its progress; already mature, and with little prospect in front of it except decay.

The diction of Anglo-Saxon poetry is a subject of study by itself. Here again there is a great difference between Anglo-Saxon and Middle English poetry. Middle English poetry borrows greatly from French. Now in all the best French poetry, with very few exceptions, the language is the same as that of prose; and even if there happen to be a few poetical words (as in Racine, for example, *flammes* and *transports* and *hymenée*) they do not interfere with the sense. Middle English generally copies French, and is generally unpretentious in its vocabulary. But Anglo-Saxon poetry was impossible without a poetical dictionary. It is very heavily ornamented with words not used in prose, and while there are hardly any similes, the whole tissue of it is figurative, and most things are named two or three times over in different terms. This makes it often very tiresome, when the meaning is so encrusted with splendid words that it can scarcely move; still more, when a poet does not take the trouble to invent his ornaments, and only repeats conventional phrases out of a vocabulary which he has learned by rote. But those extravagances of the Anglo-Saxon poetry make it all the more interesting historically; they show that there must have been a general love and appreciation of fine language, such as is not commonly found in England now, and also a technical skill in verse, something like that which is encouraged in Wales at the modern poetical competitions, though certainly far less elaborate. Further, these curiosities of old English verse make it all the more wonderful and admirable that the epic poets should have succeeded as they did with their stories of heroic resistance and the repeated waves of battle and death-agony. Tremendous subjects are easily spoilt when the literary vogue is all for ornament and fine language. Yet the Anglo-Saxon poets seldom seem to feel the encumbrances of their poetic language when they are really possessed with their subject. The eloquence of their verse then gets the better of their ornamental diction.

The subjects of Anglo-Saxon poetry were taken from many different sources besides the heroic legend which is summarized by Widsith, or contemporary actions like the battle of Maldon.

The conversion of the English to Christianity brought with it of course a great deal of Latin literature. The new ideas were adopted very readily by the English, and a hundred years after the coming of the first missionary the Northumbrian schools and teachers were more than equal to the best in any part of Europe.

The new learning did not always discourage the old native kind of poetry. Had that been the case, we should hardly have had anything like *Beowulf*; we should not have had the poem of Maldon. Christianity and Christian literature did not always banish the old-fashioned heroes. Tastes varied in this respect. The Frankish Emperor Lewis the Pious is said to have taken a disgust at the heathen poetry which he had learned when he was young. But there were greater kings who were less delicate in their religion. Charles the Great made a collection of 'the barbarous ancient poems which sung the wars and exploits of the olden time'. Alfred the Great, his Welsh biographer tells us, was always ready to listen to Saxon poems when he was a boy, and when he was older was fond of learning poetry by heart. That the poems were not all of them religious, we may see from some things in Alfred's own writings. He was bold enough to bring in a Northern hero in his translation of the Latin philosophical book of Boethius. Boethius asks, 'Where are the bones of Fabricius the true-hearted?' In place of the name Fabricius, Alfred writes, 'Where are now the bones of Wayland, and who knows where they be?' Wayland Smith, who thus appears, oddly, in the translation of Boethius, is one of the best-known heroes of the Teutonic mythology. He is the original craftsman (like Daedalus in Greece), the brother of the mythical archer Egil and the harper Slagfinn—the hero of one of the finest of the old Scandinavian poems, and of many another song and story.

The royal genealogies in the Anglo-Saxon Chronicle are an example of the conservative process that went on with regard to many of the old beliefs and fancies—a process that may be clearly traced in the poem of *Beowulf*—by means of which pre-Christian ideas were annexed to Christianity. The royal house of England, the house of Cerdic, still traces its descent from Woden; and Woden is thirteenth in descent from Noah. Woden is kept as a king and a hero, when he has ceased to be a god. This was kindlier and more charitable than the alternative view, that the gods of the heathen were living devils.

There was no destruction of the heroic poetry through the conversion of the English, but new themes were at once brought in, to compete with the old ones. Bede was born (672) within fifty years of the baptism of King Edwin of Northumbria (625), and Bede is able to tell of the poet Cædmon of Whitby who belonged to the time of the abbess Hild, between 658 and 670, and who put large portions of the Bible history into verse.

Cædmon the herdsman, turning poet late in life by a special gift from Heaven and devoting himself exclusively to sacred subjects, is a different sort of minstrel from that one who is introduced in *Beowulf* singing the lay of Finnesburh. His motive is different. It is partly the same motive as that of King Alfred in his prose translations. Cædmon made versions of Bible history for the edification of Christian people.

Anglo-Saxon poetry, which had been heathen, Teutonic, concerned with traditional heroic subjects was drawn into the service of the other world without losing its old interests. Hence comes, apart from the poetical value of the several works, the historical importance of Anglo-Saxon poetry, as a blending of *Germania*, the original Teutonic civilization, with the ideas and sentiments of Christendom in the seventh century and after.

Probably nothing of Cædmon's work remains except the first poem, which is paraphrased in Latin by Bede and which is also preserved in the original Northumbrian. But there are many Bible poems, *Genesis*, *Exodus*, and others, besides a poem on the Gospel history in the Saxon language of the Continent—the language of the 'Old Saxons', as the English called them—which followed the example and impulse given by Cædmon, and which had in common the didactic, the educational purpose, for the promotion of Christian knowledge.

But while there was this common purpose in these poems, there were as great diversities of genius as in any other literary group or school. Sometimes the author is a dull mechanical translator using the conventional forms and phrases without imagination or spirit. Sometimes on the other hand he is caught up and carried away by his subject, and the result is poetry like the *Fall of the Angels* (part of *Genesis*), or the *Dream of the Rood*. These are utterly different from the regular conventional poetry or prose of the Middle Ages. There is no harm in comparing the *Fall of the Angels* with Milton. The method is nearly the same: narrative, with a concentration on the character of Satan, and dramatic expression of the character in monologue at length. The *Dream of the Rood* again is finer than the noblest of all the Passion Plays. It is a vision, in which the Gospel history of the Crucifixion is so translated that nothing is left except the devotion of the young hero (so he is called) and the glory; it is not acted on any historical scene, but in some spiritual place where there is no distinction between the Passion and the Triumph. In this way the spirit of poetry does wonderful things; transforming the historical substance. It is quite impossible to dismiss the old English religious poetry under any summary description. Much of it is conventional and ordinary; some of it is otherwise, and the separate poems live in their own way.

It is worth remembering that the manuscripts of the *Dream of the Rood* have a history which is typical of the history in general, the progress of Anglo-Saxon poetry, and the change of centre from Northumberland to Wessex. Some verses of the poem are carved in runic letters on the Ruthwell Cross (now in the Parish Church of Ruthwell in Dumfriesshire) in the language of Northumberland, which was the language of Cædmon and Bede. The Ruthwell Cross with the runic inscription on it is thus one of the oldest poetical manuscripts in English, not to speak of its importance in other ways.

The Ruthwell verses are Northumbrian. They were at first misinterpreted in various ways by antiquaries, till John Kemble the historian read them truly. Some time after, an Anglo-Saxon manuscript was found at Vercelli in the North of Italy—a regular station on the old main road which crosses the Great St. Bernard and which was commonly used by Englishmen, Danes, and other people of the North when travelling to Rome. In this Vercelli book the *Dream of the Rood* is contained, nearly in full, but written in the language of Wessex—i.e. the language commonly called Anglo-Saxon—the language not of Bede but of Alfred. The West Saxon verses of the *Rood* corresponding to the old Anglian of the Ruthwell Cross are an example of what happened generally with Anglo-Saxon poetry—the best of it in early days was Anglian, Northumbrian; when the centre shifted to Wessex, the Northern poetry was preserved in the language which by that time had become the proper literary English both for verse and prose.

Cynewulf is an old English poet who has signed his name to several poems, extant in West Saxon. He may have been the author of the *Dream of the Rood*; he was probably a Northumbrian. As he is the most careful artist among the older poets, notable for the skill of his verse and phrasing, his poetry has to be studied attentively by any one who wishes to understand the poetical ideals of the age between Bede and King Alfred, the culmination of the Northumbrian school. His subjects are all religious, from the Gospel (*Crist*) or the lives of saints (*Guthlac, Juliana, Elene*, probably *Andreas* also). The legendary subjects may be looked on as a sort of romance; Cynewulf in many ways is a romantic poet. The adventure of St. Andrew in his voyage to rescue St. Matthew from the cannibals is told with great spirit—a story of the sea. Cynewulf has so fine a sense of the minor beauties of verse and diction that he might be in danger of losing his story for the sake of poetical ornament; but though he is not a strong poet he generally manages to avoid the temptation, and to keep the refinements of his art subordinate to the main effect.

There is hardly anything in Anglo-Saxon to be called lyrical. The epic poetry may have grown out of an older lyric type—a song in chorus, with narrative stuff in it, like the later choral ballads. There is one old poem, and a very remarkable one, with a refrain, *Deor's Lament*, which may be called a dramatic lyric, the utterance of an imaginary personage, a poet like Widsith, who comforts himself in his sorrow by recalling examples of old distresses. The burden comes after each of these records:

That ancient woe was endured, and so may mine.

Widsith in form of verse is nearer to this lyric of *Deor* than to the regular sustained narrative verse of *Beowulf*. There are some fragments of popular verse, spells against disease, which might be called songs. But what is most wanting in Anglo-Saxon literature is the sort of poetry found at the close of the Middle Ages in the popular ballads, songs and carols of the fifteenth century.

To make up for the want of true lyric, there are a few very beautiful poems, sometimes called by the name of elegies—akin to lyric, but not quite at the lyrical pitch. The *Wanderer*, the *Seafarer*, the *Ruin*, the *Wife's Complaint*—they are antique in verse and language but modern in effeçt, more than most things that come later, for many centuries. They are poems of reflective sentiment, near to the mood of a time when the bolder poetical kinds have been exhausted, and nothing is left but to refine upon the older themes. These poems are the best expression of a mood found elsewhere, even in rather early Anglo-Saxon days—the sense of the vanity of life, the melancholy regret for departed glories—a kind of thought which popular opinion calls 'the Celtic spirit', and which indeed may be found in the Ossianic poems, but not more truly than in the *Ruin* or the *Wanderer*.

When the language of Wessex became the literary English, it was naturally used for poetry—not merely for translations of Northumbrian verse into West Saxon. The strange thing about this later poetry is that it should be capable of such strength as is shown in the Maldon poem—a perpetual warning against rash conclusions. For poetry had seemed to be exhausted long before this, or at any rate to have reached in Cynewulf the dangerous stage of maturity. But the Maldon poem, apart from some small technical faults, is sane and strong. In contrast, the earlier poem in the battle of Brunanburh is a fair conventional piece—academic laureate work, using cleverly enough the forms which any accomplished gentleman could learn.

Those forms are applied often most ingeniously, in the Anglo-Saxon riddles; pieces, again, which contradict ordinary opinion. Few would expect to find in Anglo-Saxon the curious grace of verbal workmanship, the artificial wit, of those short poems.

The dialogue of *Salomon and Saturnus* is one of the Anglo-Saxon things belonging to a common European fashion; the dialogue literature, partly didactic, partly comic, which was so useful in the Middle Ages in providing instruction along with varying degrees of amusement. There is more than one Anglo-Saxon piece of this sort, valuable as expressing the ordinary mind; for, generally speaking, there is a want of merely popular literature in Anglo-Saxon, as compared with the large amount later on.

The history of prose is continuous from the Anglo-Saxon onwards; there is no such division as between Anglo-Saxon and Middle English poetry. In fact, Middle English prose at first is the continuation of the English Chronicle, and the transcription of the homilies of Ælfric into the later grammar and spelling.

The English had not the peculiar taste for prose which seems to be dealt by chance to Hebrews and Arabs, to Ireland and Iceland. As in Greece and France, the writing of prose comes after verse. It begins by being useful; it is not used for heroic stories. But the English had more talent for prose than some people; they understood it better than the French; and until the French influence came over them did not habitually degrade their verse for merely useful purposes.

Through the Chronicle, which probably began in King Alfred's time, and through Alfred's translations from the Latin, a common available prose was established, which had all sorts of possibilities in it, partly realized after a time. There seems no reason, as far as language and technical ability are concerned, why there should not have been in English, prose stories as good as those of Iceland. The episode of King Cynewulf of Wessex, in the Chronicle, has been compared to the Icelandic sagas, and to the common epic theme of valorous fighting and loyal perseverance. In Alfred's narrative passages there are all the elements of plain history, a style that might have been used without limit for all the range of experience.

Alfred's prose when he is repeating the narratives of his sea-captains has nothing in it that can possibly weary, so long as the subject is right. It is a perfectly clean style for matter of fact.

The great success of Anglo-Saxon prose is in religious instruction. This is various in kind; it includes the translation of Boethius which is philosophy, and fancy as well; it includes the Dialogues of Gregory which are popular stories, the homilies on Saints' Lives which are often prose romances, and which often are heightened above prose, into a swelling, chanting, alliterative tune, not far from the language of poetry. The great master of prose in all its forms is Ælfric of Eynsham, about the year 1000. Part of his work was translation of the Bible, and in this, and in his theory of translation, he is more enlightened than any translator before Tyndale. The fault of Bible versions generally was that they kept too close to the original. Instead of translating like free men they construed word for word, like the illiterate in all ages. Ulphilas, who is supposed by some to have written Gothic prose, is really a slave to the Greek text, and his Gothic is hardly a human language. Wycliffe treats his Latin original in the same way, and does not think what language he is supposed to be writing. But Ælfric works on principles that would have been approved by Dryden; and there is no better evidence of the humanities in those early times than this. Much was lost before the work of Ælfric was taken up again with equal intelligence.

3

The Middle English Period (1150–1500)

Introductory

ANGLO-SAXON AND Middle English literature had many things in
common. The educational work of King Alfred was continued all
through the Middle Ages. Chaucer translates Boethius, five hundred
years after King Alfred's translation. The same authors are read and
adapted. The sermons of Ælfric, A.D. 1000, have the same sort of
matter as those of the thirteenth or the fourteenth century, and there
is no very great difference of tone. Many of the literary interests of
the Plantagenet times are found already among the Anglo-Saxons.
The Legends of the Saints are inexhaustible subjects of poetical treatment in the earlier as well as the later days. The poetical expression
is, of course, very greatly changed, but earlier or later the Saints'
Lives are used as material for literature which is essentially romantic,
whatever its other qualities may be. There are other sources of
romance open, long before the French influence begins to be felt in
England; particularly, the wonders of the East appear in the Anglo-
Saxon version of Alexander's letter to Aristotle; and later Greek
romance (through the Latin) in the Anglo-Saxon translation of
Apollonius of Tyre.

The great difference between the two ages is made by the dis-
appearance of the old English poetry. There is nothing in the Plantagenet reigns like *Beowulf* or the Maldon poem; there is nothing
like the *Fall of the Angels* and the dramatic eloquence of Satan. The
pathos of the later Middle Ages is expressed in a different way from
the *Wanderer* and the *Ruin*. The later religious poetry has little in it

MEL—B

to recall the finished art of Cynewulf. Anglo-Saxon poetry, whether derived from heathendom or from the Church, has ideas and manners of its own; it comes to perfection, and then it dies away. The gravity and thought of the heroic poetry, as well as the finer work of the religious poets, are unlike the strength, unlike the graces, of the later time. Anglo-Saxon poetry grows to a rich maturity, and past it; then, with the new forms of language and under new influences, the poetical education has to start again.

Unfortunately for the historian, there are scarcely any literary things remaining to show the progress of the transition. For a long time before and after 1100 there is a great scarcity of English productions. It is not till about 1200 that Middle English literature begins to be at all fully represented.

This scantiness is partly due, no doubt, to an actual disuse of English composition. But many written things must have perished, and in poetry there was certainly a large amount of verse current orally, whether it was ever written down or not. This is the inference drawn from the passages in the historian William of Malmesbury to which Macaulay refers in his preface to the *Lays of Ancient Rome*, and which Freeman has studied in his essay on *The Mythical and Romantic Elements in Early English History*. The story of Hereward the Wake is extant in Latin; the story of Havelock the Dane and others were probably composed in English verse much earlier than the thirteenth century, and in much older forms than those which have come down to us.

There is a gap in the record of alliterative poetry which shows plainly that much has been lost. It is a curious history. Before the Norman conquest the old English verse had begun to go to pieces, in spite of such excellent late examples as the Maldon poem. About 1200 the alliterative verse, though it has still something of its original character, is terribly broken down. The verse of Layamon's *Brut* is unsteady, never to be trusted, changing its pace without warning in a most uncomfortable way. Then suddenly, as late as the middle of the fourteenth century, there begins a procession of magnificent alliterative poems, in regular verse—*Sir Gawayne,* the *Morte Arthure*, *Piers Plowman*; in regular verse, not exactly with the same rule as *Beowulf*, but with so much of the old rule as seemed to have been hopelessly lost for a century or two. What is the explanation of this revival, and this sudden great vogue of alliterative poetry? It cannot have been a new invention, or a reconstruction; it would not in that case have copied, as it sometimes does, the rhythm of the old English verse in a way which is unlike the ordinary rhythms of the fourteenth century. The only reasonable explanation is that somewhere in England there was a tradition of alliterative verse, keeping in the main to the old rules of rhythm as it kept something of the old vocabulary, and escaping the disease which affected the old verse elsewhere. The purer sort of verse must have been preserved for a few hundred years with hardly a trace of it among the existing documents to show what it was like till it breaks out 'three-score thousand strong' in the reign of Edward III.

In the Middle Ages, early and late, there was very free communication all over Christendom between people of different languages. Languages seem to have given much less trouble than they do nowadays. The general use of Latin, of course, made things easy for those who could speak it; but without Latin, people of different nations appear to have travelled over the world picking up foreign languages as they went along, and showing more interest in the poetry and stories of foreign countries than is generally found among modern tourists. Luther said of the people of Flanders that if you took a Fleming in a sack and carried him over France or Italy, he would manage to learn the tongues. This gift was useful to commercial travellers, and perhaps the Flemings had more of it than other people. But in all the nations there seems to have been something like this readiness, and in all it was used to translate the stories and adapt the poetry of other tongues. This intercourse was greatly quickened in the twelfth century through a number of causes, the principal cause being the extraordinary production of new poetry in France, or rather in the two regions, North and South, and the two languages, French and Provençal. Between these two languages, in the North and the South of what is now France, there was in the Middle Ages a kind of division of labour. The North took narrative poetry, the South took lyric; and French narrative and Provençal lyric poetry in the twelfth century between them made the beginning of modern literature for the whole of Europe.

In the earlier Middle Ages, before 1100, as in the later, the common language is Latin. Between the Latin authors of the earlier time—Gregory the Great, or Bede—and those of the later—Anselm, or Thomas Aquinas—there may be great differences, but there is no line of separation.

In the literature of the native tongues there is a line of division about 1100 more definite than any later epoch; it is made by the appearance of French poetry, bringing along with it an intellectual unity of Christendom which has never been shaken since.

The importance of this is that it meant a mutual understanding among the laity of Europe, equal to that which had so long obtained among the clergy, the learned men.

The year 1100, in which all Christendom is united, if not thoroughly and actively in all places, for the conquest of the Holy Sepulchre, at any rate ideally by the thought of this common enterprise, is also a year from which may be dated the beginning of the common lay intelligence of Europe, that sympathy of understanding by which ideas of different sorts are taken up and diffused, outside of the professionally learned bodies. The year 1100 is a good date, because of the first Provençal poet, William, Count of Poitiers, who was living then; he went on the Crusade three years later. He is the first poet of modern Europe who definitely helps to set a fashion of poetry not only for his own people but for the imitation of foreigners. He is the first modern poet; he uses the kind of verse which every one uses now.

The triumph of French poetry in the twelfth century was the end of the old Teutonic world—an end which had been long preparing, though it came suddenly at last. Before that time there had been the sympathy and informal union among the Germanic nations out of which the old heroic poems had come; such community of ideas as allowed the Nibelung story to be treated in all the Germanic tongues from Austria to Iceland, and even in Greenland, the furthest outpost of the Northmen. But after the eleventh century there was nothing new to be got out of this. Here and there may be found a gleaner, like Saxo Grammaticus, getting together all that he can save out of the ancient heathendom, or like the Norwegian traveller about fifty years later, who collected North German ballads of Theodoric and other champions, and paraphrased them in Norwegian prose. The really great achievement of the older world in its last days was in the prose histories of Iceland, which had virtue enough in them to change the whole world, if they had only been known and understood; but they were written for domestic circulation, and even their own people scarcely knew how good they were. Germania was falling to pieces, the separate nations growing more and more stupid and drowsy.

The languages derived from Latin—commonly called the Romance languages—French and Provençal, Italian and so on— were long of declaring themselves. The Italian and Spanish dialects had to wait for the great French outburst before they could produce anything. French and Provençal, which are well in front of Spanish and Italian, have little of importance to show before 1100. But after that date there is such profusion that it is clear there had been a long time of experiment and preparation. The earlier French epics have been lost; the earliest known Provençal poet is already a master of verse, and must be indebted to many poetical ancestors whose names and poems have disappeared. Long before 1100 there must have been a common literary taste in France, fashions of poetry well under- stood and appreciated, a career open for youthful poets. In the twelfth century the social success of poetry in France was extended in different degrees over all Europe. In Italy and Spain the fashions were taken up; in Germany they conquered even more quickly and thoroughly; the Danes and Swedes and Norwegians learned their ballad measures from the French; even the Icelanders, the only Northern nation with a classical literature and with minds of their own, were caught in the same way.

Thus French poetry wakened up the sleepy countries, and gave new ideas to the wakeful; it brought the Teutonic and Romance nations to agree and, what was much more important, to produce new works of their own which might be original in all sorts of ways while still keeping within the limits of the French tradition. Com- pared with this, all later literary revolutions are secondary and partial changes. The most widely influential writers of later ages— e.g. Petrarch and Voltaire—had the ground prepared for them in this medieval epoch, and do nothing to alter the general conditions which were then established—the inter-communication among the whole laity of Europe with regard to questions of taste.

It seems probable that the Normans had a good deal to do as agents in this revolution. They were in relation with many different people. They had Bretons on their borders in Normandy; they conquered England, and then they touched upon the Welsh; they were fond of pilgrimages; they settled in Apulia and Sicily, where they had dealings with Greeks and Saracens as well as Italians.

It is a curious thing that early in the twelfth century names are found in Italy which certainly come from the romances of King Arthur—the name Galvano, e.g. which is the same as Gawain. However it was brought there, this name may be taken for a sign of the process that was going on everywhere—the conversion of Europe to fashions which were prescribed in France.

The narrative poetry in which the French excelled was of different kinds. An old French poet, in an epic on Charlemagne's wars against the Saxons, has given a classification which is well known, dividing the stories according to the historical matter which they employ. There are three 'matters', he says, and no more than three, which a story-teller may take up—the matter of France, the matter of Britain, the matter of Rome the Great. The old poet is right in naming these as at any rate the chief groups; since 'Rome the Great' might be made to take in whatever would not go into the other two divisions, there is nothing much wrong in his refusal to make a fourth class. The 'matter of France' includes all the subjects of the old French national epics—such as Roncevaux, or the song of Roland; Reynold of Montalban, or the Four Sons of Aymon; Ferabras; Ogier the Dane. The matter of Britain includes all the body of the Arthurian legend, as well as the separate stories commonly called Breton lays (like Chaucer's Franklin's Tale). The matter of Rome is not only Roman history, but the whole of classical antiquity. The story of Troy, of course, is rightly part of Roman history, and so is the romance of Eneas. But under Rome the Great there fall other stories which have much slighter connexion with Rome—such as the story of Thebes, or of Alexander.

Many of those subjects were of course well known and popular before the French poets took them up. The romantic story of Alexander might, in part at any rate, have been familiar to Alfred the Great; he brings the Egyptian king 'Nectanebus the wizard' into his translation of Orosius—Nectanebus, who is the father of Alexander in the apocryphal book from which the romances were derived. But it was not till the French poets turned the story of Alexander into verse that it really made much impression outside of France. The tale of Troy was widely read, in various authors—Ovid and Virgil, and an abstract of the *Iliad*, and in the apocryphal prose books of Dares the Phrygian and Dictys the Cretan, who were supposed to have been at the seat of war, and therefore to be better witnesses than Homer. These were used and translated sometimes apart from any French suggestion. But it was the French *Roman de Troie*, written in the twelfth century, which spread the story everywhere—the source of innumerable Troy Books in all languages, and of Chaucer's and Shakespeare's *Troilus*.

The 'matter of Britain' also was generally made known through the works of French authors. There are exceptions; the British history of Geoffrey of Monmouth was written in Latin. But even this found its way into English by means of a French translation; the *Brut* of Layamon, a long poem in irregular alliterative verse, is adapted from a French rhyming translation of Geoffrey's History. The English romances of Sir Perceval, Sir Gawain and other knights are founded on French poems.

There is an important distinction between the 'matter of France' and the 'matters' of Britain and Rome; this distinction belongs more properly to the history of French literature, but it ought not to be neglected here. The 'matter of France', which is exemplified in the song of Roland, belongs to an earlier time, and was made into French poetry earlier than the other subjects. The poems about Charlemagne and his peers, and others of the same sort, are sometimes called the old French epics; the French name for them is *chansons de geste*. Those epics have not only a different matter but a different form from the French Arthurian romances and the French *Roman de Troie*. What is of more importance for English poetry, there is generally a different tone and sentiment. They are older, stronger, more heroic, more like *Beowulf* or the Maldon poem; the romances of the 'matter of Britain', on the other hand, are the fashionable novels of the twelfth century; their subjects are really taken from contemporary polite society. They are long love-stories, and their motive chiefly is to represent the fortunes, and, above all, the sentiments of true lovers.

Roughly speaking, the 'matter of France' is action, the 'matter of Britain' is sentiment. The 'matter of Rome' is mixed; for while the *Roman de Troie* (with the love-story of Troilus, and with courteous modern manners throughout) is like the romances of Lancelot and Tristram, Alexander, in the French versions, is a hero like those of the national epics, and is celebrated in the same manner as Charlemagne.

The 'matter of France' could not be popular in England as it was in its native country. But Charlemagne and Roland and his peers were well known everywhere, like Arthur and Alexander, and the 'matter of France' went to increase the stories told by English minstrels. It was from an English version, in the thirteenth century, that part of the long Norwegian prose history of Charlemagne was taken; a fact worth remembering, to illustrate the way in which the exportation of stories was carried on. Of course, the story of Charlemagne was not the same sort of thing in England or Norway that it was in France. The devotion of France which is so intense in the song of Roland was never meant to be shared by any foreigner. But Roland as a champion against the infidels was a hero everywhere. There are statues of him in Bremen and in Verona; and it is in Italy that the story is told of the simple man who was found weeping in the market-place; a professional story-teller had just come to the death of Roland and the poor man heard the news for the first time. A traveller in the Faroe Islands not long ago, asking in the bookshop at Thorshavn for some things in the Faroese language, was offered a ballad of Roncesvalles.

The favourite story everywhere was *Sir Ferabras*, because the centre of the plot is the encounter between Oliver the Paladin and Ferebras the Paynim champion. Every one could understand this, and in all countries the story became popular as a sound religious romance.

Naturally, the stories of action and adventure went further and were more widely appreciated than the cultivated sentimental romance. The English in the reign of Edward I or Edward III had often much difficulty in understanding what the French romantic school was driving at—particularly when it seemed to be driving round and round, spinning long monologues of afflicted damsels, or elegant conversations full of phrases between the knight and his lady. The difficulty was not unreasonable. If the French authors had been content to write about nothing but sentimental conversations and languishing lovers, then one would have known what to do. The man who is looking at the railway bookstall for a good detective story knows at once what to say when he is offered the Diary of a Soul. But the successful French novelists of the twelfth century appealed to both tastes, and dealt equally in sensation and sentiment; they did not often limit themselves to what was always their chief interest, the moods of lovers. They worked these into plots of adventure, mystery, fairy magic; the adventures were too good to be lost; so the less refined English readers, who were puzzled or wearied by sentimental conversations, were not able to do without the elegant romances. They read them; and they skipped. The skipping was done for them, generally, when the romances were translated into English; the English versions are shorter than the French in most cases where comparison is possible. As a general rule, the English took the adventurous sensational part of the French romances, and let the language of the heart alone. To this there are exceptions. In the first place it is not always true that the French romances are adventurous. Some of them are almost purely love-stories—sentiment from beginning to end. Further, it is proved that one of these, *Amadas et Ydoine*—a French romance written in England—was much liked in England by many whose proper language was English; there is no English version of it extant, and perhaps there never was one, but it was certainly well known outside the limited refined society for which is was composed. And again there may be found examples where the English adapter, instead of skipping, sets himself to wrestle with the original—saying to himself, 'I will *not* be beaten by this culture; I will get to the end of it and lose nothing; it shall be made to go into the English language'. An example of this effort is the alliterative romance of *William and the Werwolf*, a work which does not fulfil the promise of its title in any satisfactory way. It spends enormous trouble over the sentimental passages of the original, turning them into the form worst suited to them, viz. the emphatic style of the alliterative poetry which is so good for battle pieces, satire, storms at sea, and generally everything except what it is here applied to. Part of the success of Chaucer and almost all the beauty of Gower may be said to be their mastery of French polite literature, and their power of expressing in English everything that could be said in French, with no loss of effect and no inferiority in manner. Gower ought to receive his due alongside of Chaucer as having accomplished what many English writers had attempted for two hundred years before him—the perfect adoption in English verse of everything remarkable in the style of French poetry.

The history of narrative poetry is generally easier than the history of lyric, partly because the subjects are more distinct and more easily traceable. But it is not difficult to recognize the enormous difference between the English songs of the fourteenth century and anything known to us in Anglo-Saxon verse, while the likeness of English to French lyrical measures in the later period is unquestionable. The difficulty is that the history of early French lyric poetry is itself obscure and much more complicated than the history of narrative. Lyric poetry flourished at popular assemblies and festivals, and was kept alive in oral tradition much more easily than narrative poetry was. Less of it, in proportion, was written down, until it was taken up by ambitious poets and composed in a more elaborate way.

The distinction between popular and cultivated lyric is not always easy to make out, as any one may recognize who thinks of the songs of Burns and attempts to distinguish what is popular in them from what is consciously artistic. But the distinction is a sound one, and especially necessary in the history of medieval literature—all the more because the two kinds often pass into one another.

A good example is the earliest English song, as it is sometimes called, which is very far from the earliest—

> Sumer is icumen in
> lhude sing cuccu.

It sounds like a popular song; an anonymous poem from the heart of the people, in simple, natural, spontaneous verse. But look at the original copy. The song is written, of course, for music. And the Cuckoo song is said by the historians of music to be remarkable and novel; it is the first example of a canon; it is not an improvisation, but the newest kind of art, one of the most ingenious things of its time. Further, the words that belong to it are Latin words, a Latin hymn; the Cuckoo song, which appears so natural and free, is the result of deliberate study; syllable for syllable, it corresponds to the Latin, and to the notes of the music.

Is it then *not* to be called a popular song? Perhaps the answer is that all popular poetry, in Europe at any rate for the last thousand years, is derived from poetry more or less learned in character, or, like the Cuckoo song, from more or less learned music. The first popular songs of the modern world were the hymns of St. Ambrose, and the oldest fashion of popular tunes is derived from the music of the Church.

The learned origin of popular lyric may be illustrated from any of the old-fashioned broadsheets of the street ballad-singers: for example *The Kerry Recruit*—

> As I was going up and down, one day in the month of August,
> All in the town of sweet Tralee, I met the recruiting serjeant—

The metre of this is the same as in the *Ormulum*—

> This book is nemned Ormulum, for thy that Orm hit wroughtè.

It is derived through the Latin from the Greek; it was made popular first through Latin rhyming verses which were imitated in the vernacular languages, Provençal, German, English. As it is a variety of 'common metre', it is easily fitted to popular tunes, and so it becomes a regular type of verse, both for ambitious poets and for ballad-minstrels like the author quoted above. It may be remembered that a country poet wrote the beautiful song on Yarrow from which Wordsworth took the verse of his own Yarrow poems—

> But minstrel Burne cannot assuage
> His grief, while life endureth,
> To see the changes of this age
> Which fleeting time procureth—

verse identical in measure with the *Ormulum*, and with the popular

Irish street ballad, and with many more. So in the history of this type of verse we get the following relations of popular and literary poetry: first there is the ancient Greek verse of the same measure; then there are the Latin learned imitations; then there is the use of it by scholars in the Middle Ages, who condescend to use it in Latin rhymes for students' choruses. Then comes the imitation of it in different languages as in English by Orm and others of his day (about 1200). It was very much in favour then, and was used often irregularly, with a varying number of syllables. But Orm writes it with perfect accuracy, and the accurate type survived, and was just as 'popular' as the less regular kind. Minstrel Burne is as regular as the *Ormulum*, and so, or very nearly as much, is the anonymous Irish poet of *The Kerry Recruit*.

What happened in the case of the *Ormulum* verse is an example of the whole history of modern lyric poetry in its earlier period. Learned men like St. Ambrose and St. Augustine wrote hymns for the common people in Latin which the common people of that time could understand. Then, in different countries, the native languages were used to copy the Latin measures and fit in to the same tunes —just as the English Cuckoo song corresponds to the Latin words for the same melody. Thus there were provided for the new languages, as we may call them, a number of poetical forms or patterns which could be applied in all sorts of ways. These became common and well understood, in the same manner as common forms of music are understood, e.g. the favourite rhythms of dance tunes; and like those rhythms they could be adapted to any sort of poetical subject, and used with all varieties of skill.

Many strange things happened while the new rhyming sort of lyric poetry was being acclimatized in England, and a study of early English lyrics is a good introduction to all the rest of English poetry, because in those days—in the twelfth and thirteenth centuries—may be found the origin of the most enduring poetical influences in later times.

One of the strange things was that the French lyrical examples affected the English in two opposite ways. As foreign verse, and as belonging especially to those who were acquainted with courts and good society, it had the attraction which fashionable and stylish things generally have for those who are a little behind the fashion. It was the newest and most brilliant thing; the English did all they could to make it their own whether by composing in French themselves or by copying the French style in English words. But besides this fashionable and courtly value of French poetry, there was another mode in which it appealed to the English. Much of it was closely related not to the courts but to popular country festivals which were frequent also in towns, like the games and dances to celebrate the coming of May. French poetry was associated with games of that sort, and along with games of that sort it came to England. The English were hit on both sides. French poetry was more genteel in some things, more popular and jovial in others, than anything then current in England. Thus the same foreign mode of composition which gave a new courtly ideal to the English helped also very greatly to quicken their popular life. While the distinction between courtly and popular is nowhere more important than in medieval literature, it is often very hard to make it definite in particular cases, just for this reason. It is not as if there were a popular native layer, English in character and origin, with a courtly foreign French layer above it. What is popular in Middle English literature is just as much French as English; while, on the other hand, what is native, like the alliterative verse, is as often as not used for ambitious works. *Sir Gawayne and the Greene Knight* and the poem of the *Morte Arthure* are certainly not 'popular' in the sense of 'uneducated' or 'simple' or anything of that kind, and though they are written in the old native verse they are not intended for the people who had no education and could not speak French.

The great manifestation of French influence in the common life of the Middle Ages was through the fashion of the dance which generally went by the name of *Carole*. The *carole*—music, verse and dance altogether—spread as a fashion all over Europe in the twelfth century; and there is nothing which so effectively marks the change from the earlier to the later Middle Ages. It *is* in fact a great part of the change, with all that is implied in it; which may be explained in the following way.

The *carole* was a dance accompanied by a song, the song being divided between a leader and the rest of the chorus; the leader sang

the successive new lines, while the rest of the dancers holding hands
in a ring all joined in the refrain. Now this was the fashion most in
favour in all gentle houses through the Middle Ages, and it was
largely through this that the French type of lyric was transported to
so many countries and languages. French lyric poetry was part of a
graceful diversion for winter evenings in a castle or for summer
afternoons in the castle garden. But it was also thoroughly and
immediately available for all the parish. In its origin it was popular
in the widest sense—not restricted to any one rank or class; and
though it was adopted and elaborated in the stately homes of
England and other countries it could not lose its original character.
Every one could understand it and enjoy it; so it became the
favourite thing at popular festivals, as well as at the Christmas enter-
tainments in the great hall. Particularly, it was a favourite custom to
dance and sing in this way on the vigils or eves of Saints' days, when
people assembled from some distance at the church where the day
was to be observed. Dancing-parties were frequent at these 'wakes';
they were often held in the churchyard. There are many stories to
show how they were discouraged by the clergy, and how deplorable
was their vanity; but those moral examples also prove how well
established the custom was; some of them also from their date show
how quickly it had spread. The best is in Giraldus Cambrensis,
'Gerald the Welshman', a most amusing writer, who is unfortunately little read, as he wrote in Latin. In his *Gemma Ecclesiastica* he
has a chapter against the custom of using churches and churchyards
for songs and dances. As an illustration, he tells the story of a wake
in a churchyard, somewhere in the diocese of Worcester, which was
kept up all night long, the dancers repeating one refrain over and
over; so that the priest who had this refrain in his ears all night
could not get rid of it in the morning, but repeated it at the Mass—
saying (instead of *Dominus vobiscum*) 'Sweet Heart, have pity!'
Giraldus, writing in Latin, quotes the English verse: *Swete
lemman, thin arè. Are*, later *ore*, means 'mercy' or 'grace', and the
refrain is of the same sort as is found, much later, in the lyric poetry
of the time of Edward I. Giraldus wrote in the twelfth century, in
the reign of Henry II, and it is plain from what he tells that the
French fashion was already in full swing and as thoroughly

naturalized among the English as the Waltz or the Lancers in the nineteenth century. The same sort of evidence comes from Denmark about the same time as Giraldus; ring-dances were equally a trouble and vexation to religious teachers there—for, strangely, the dances seem everywhere to have been drawn to churches and monasteries, through the custom of keeping religious wakes in a cheerful manner. Europe was held together in this common vanity, and it was through the *caroles* and similar amusements that the poetical art of France came to be dominant all over the North, affecting the popular and unpretending poets no less than those of greater ambition and conceit.

The word 'Court' and its derivations are frequently used by medieval and early modern writers with a special reference to poetry. The courts of kings and great nobles were naturally associated with the ideas of polite education; those men 'that has used court and dwelled therein can Frankis and Latin', says Richard Rolle of Hampole in the fourteenth century; the 'courtly maker' is an Elizabethan name for the accomplished poet, and similar terms are used in other languages to express the same meaning. This 'courtly' ideal was not properly realized in England till the time of Chaucer and Gower; and a general view of the subject easily leads one to think of the English language as struggling in the course of three centuries to get rid of its homeliness, its rustic and parochial qualities. This period, from about 1100 to 1400, closes in the full attainment of the desired end. Chaucer and Gower are unimpeachable as 'courtly makers', and their success in this way also implies the establishment of their language as pure English; the competition of dialects is ended by the victory of the East Midland language which Chaucer and Gower used. The 'courtly poets' make it impossible in England to use any language for poetry except their own.

But the distinction between 'courtly' and 'vulgar', 'popular', or whatever the other term may be, is not very easy to fix. The history of the *carole* is an example of this difficulty. The *carole* flourishes among the gentry and it is a favourite amusement as well among the common people. 'Courtly' ideas, suggestions, phrases, might have a circulation in country places, and be turned to literary effect by authors who had no special attachment to good society. A hundred years before Chaucer there may be found in the poem of *The Owl and the Nightingale*, written in the language of Dorset, a kind of good-humoured ironical satire which is very like Chaucer's own. This is the most *modern* in tone of all the thirteenth-century poems, but there are many others in which the rustic, or popular, and the 'courtly' elements are curiously and often very pleasantly mixed.

In fact, for many purposes even of literary history and criticism the medieval distinction between 'courtly' and popular may be neglected. There is always a difficulty in finding out what is meant by 'the People'. One has only to remember Chaucer's Pilgrims to understand this, and to realize how absurd is any fixed line of division between ranks, with regard to their literary taste. The most attentive listener and the most critical among the Canterbury Pilgrims is the Host of the Tabard. There was 'culture' in the Borough as well as in Westminster. The Franklin who apologizes for his want of rhetorical skill—he had never read Tullius or Cicero —tells one of the 'Breton lays', a story elegantly planned and finished, of the best French type; and the Wife of Bath, after the story of her own life, repeats another romance of the same school as the Franklin's Tale. The average 'reading public' of Chaucer's time could understand a great many different varieties of verse and prose.

But while the difference between 'courtly' and 'popular' is often hard to determine in particular cases, it is none the less important and significant in medieval history. It implies the chivalrous ideal— the self-conscious withdrawal and separation of the gentle folk from all the rest, not merely through birth and rank and the fashion of their armour, but through their ways of thinking, and especially through their theory of love. The devotion of the true knight to his lady—the motive of all the books of chivalry—began to be the favourite subject in the twelfth century; it was studied and medi- tated in all manner of ways, and it is this that gives its character to all the most original, as well as to the most artificial, poetry of the later Middle Ages. The spirit and the poetical art of the different nations may be estimated according to the mode in which they appropriated those ideas. For the ideas of this religion of chivalrous love were *literary* and *artistic* ideas; they went along with poetical ambitions and the fresh poetical invention—they led to the poetry of Dante, Petrarch and Spenser, not as ideas and inspirations simply, but through their employment of definite poetical forms of expression, which were developed by successive generations of poets.

Stories of true love do not belong peculiarly to the age of chivalrous romance. The greatest of them all, the story of Sigurd and Brynhild, has come down from an older world. The early books of the Danish History of Saxo Grammaticus are full of romantic themes. 'A mutual love arose between Hedin and Hilda, the daughter of Hogne, a maiden of most eminent renown. For though they had not yet seen one another, each had been kindled by the other's glory. But when they had a chance of beholding one another, neither could look away; so steadfast was the love that made their eyes linger.' This passage (quoted from Oliver Elton's translation) is one of the things which were collected by Saxo from Danish tradition; it is quite independent of anything chivalrous, in the special sense of that word. Again, Chaucer's *Legend of Good Women*, the story of Dido, or of Pyramus and Thisbe, may serve as a reminder how impossible it is to separate 'romantic' from 'classical' literature. A great part of medieval romance is nothing but a translation into medieval forms, into French couplets, of the passion of Medea or of Dido. Even in the fresh discovery which made the ideal of the 'courtly' schools, namely, the lover's worship of his lady as divine, there is something traceable to the Latin poets. But it was a fresh discovery, for all that, a new mode of thought, whatever its source might be. The devotion of Dante to Beatrice, of Petrarch to Laura, is different from anything in classical poetry, or in the earlier Middle Ages. It is first in Provençal lyric verse that something like their ideas may be found; both Dante and Petrarch acknowledge their debt to the Provençal poets.

Those ideas can be expressed in lyric poetry; not so well in narrative. They are too vague for narrative, and too general; they are the utterance of any true lover, his pride and his humility, his belief that all the joy and grace of the world, and of Heaven also, are included in the worshipful lady. There is also along with this religion a firm belief that it is not intended for the vulgar; and as the ideas and motives are noble so must the poetry be, in every respect. The refinement of the idea requires a corresponding beauty of form; and the lyric poets of Provence and their imitators in Germany, the Minnesingers, were great inventors of new stanzas and, it should be remembered, of the tunes that accompanied them. It was not allowable for one poet to take another poet's stanza. The new spirit of devotion in love-poetry produced an enormous variety of lyrical measures, which are still musical, and some of them still current, to this day.

It was an artificial kind of poetry, in different senses of the term. It was consciously artistic, and ambitious; based upon science—the science of music—and deliberately planned so as to make the best effect. The poets were competitors—sometimes in actual competition for a prize, as in the famous scene at the Wartburg, which comes in *Tannhäuser*, or as at a modern Welsh *eisteddfod*; the fame of a poet could not be gained without the finest technical skill, and the prize was often given for technical skill, rather than for anything else. Besides this, the ideas themselves were conventional; the poet's amatory religion was often assumed; he chose a lady to whom he offered his poetical homage. The fiction was well understood, and was hightly appreciated as an honour, when the poetry was success-ful. For example, the following may be taken from the Lives of the Troubadours—

'Richard of Barbezieux the poet fell in love with a lady, the wife of a noble lord. She was gentle and fair, and gay and gracious, and very desirous of praise and honour; daughter of Jeffrey Rudel, prince of Blaye. And when she knew that he loved her, she made him fair semblance of love, so that he got hardihood to plead his suit to her. And she with gracious countenance of love treasured his praise of her, and accepted and listened, as a lady who had good will of a poet to make verses about her. And he composed his songs of her, and called her *Mielhs de Domna* ("Sovran Lady") in his verse. And he took great delight in finding similitudes of beasts and birds and men in his poetry, and of the sun and the stars, so as to give new arguments such as no poet had found before him. Long time he sang to her; but it was never believed that she yielded to his suit.'

Provençal poetry cannot be shown to have had any direct influence upon English, which is rather strange considering the close relations between England and the districts where the Provençal language— the *langue d'oc*—was spoken. It had great indirect influence, through the French. The French imitated the Provençal lyric poetry, as the Germans and the Italians did, and by means of the French poets the Provençal ideas found their way to England. But this took a long time. The Provençal poets were 'courtly makers'; so were the French who copied them. The 'courtly maker' needs not only great houses and polite society for his audience; not only the fine philosophy 'the love of honour and the honour of love', which is the foundation of chivalrous romance. Besides all this, he needs the reward and approbation of success in poetical art; he cannot thrive as an anonymous poet. And it is not till the time of Chaucer and Gower that there is found in England any poet making a great name for himself as a master of the art of poetry, like the Provençal masters Bernart de Ventadour or Arnaut Daniel in the twelfth century, or like the German Walther von der Vogelweide at the beginning of the thirteenth.

Lyric poetry of the Provençal kind was a most exacting and difficult art; it required very peculiar conditions before it could flourish and be appreciated, and those conditions did not exist in England or in the English language. At the same time the elaborate lyrics of Provence, like those of the Minnesingers in Germany, are pretty closely related to many 'popular' forms and motives. Besides the idealist love-poetry there were other kinds available—simple songs of lament, or of satire—comic songs—lyrics with a scene in them, such as the very beautiful one about the girl whose lover had gone on the Crusade. In such as these, though they have little directly to do with English poetry, may be found many illustrations of English modes of verse, and rich examples of that most delightful sort of poetry which refuses to be labelled either 'courtly' or 'popular'.

In French literature, as distinct from Provençal, there was a 'courtly' strain which flourished in the same general conditions as the Provençal, but was not so hard to understand and had a much greater immediate effect on England.

The French excelled in narrative poetry. There seems to have been a regular exchange in poetry between the South and the North of France. French stories were translated into Provençal, Provençal lyrics were imitated in the North of France. Thus French lyric is partly Provençal in character, and it is in this way that the Provençal influence is felt in English poetry. The French narrative poetry, though it also is affected by ideas from the South, is properly French in origin and style. It is by means of narrative that the French ideal of courtesy and chivalry is made known, to the French themselves as well as to other nations.

In the twelfth century a considerable change was made in French poetry by the rise and progress of a new romantic school in succession to the old *chansons de geste*—the epic poems on the 'matter of France'. The old epics went down in the world, and gradually passed into the condition of merely 'popular' literature. Some of them survive to this day in roughly printed editions, like the *Reali di Francia*, which is an Italian prose paraphrase of old French epics, and which seems to have a good sale in the markets of Italy still, as *The Seven Champions of Christendom* used to have in England, and *The Four Sons of Aymon* in France. The decline of the old epics began in the twelfth century through the competition of more brilliant new romances.

The subjects of these were generally taken either from the 'matter of Britain', or from antiquity, the 'matter of Rome the Great', which included Thebes and Troy. The new romantic school wanted new subjects, and by preference foreign subjects. This, however, was of comparatively small importance; it had long been usual for story-tellers to go looking for subjects to foreign countries; this is proved by the Saints' Lives, and also by the story of Alexander the Great, which appeared in French before the new school was properly begun.

In form of verse the new romances generally differed from the *chansons de geste*, but this again is not an exact distinction. Apart from other considerations, the distinction fails because the octo-syllabic rhyming measure, the short couplet, which was the ordinary form for fashionable romances, was also at the same time the ordinary form for everything else—for history, for moral and didactic poetry, and for comic stories like Reynard the Fox. The establishment of this 'short verse' (as the author of *Hudibras* calls it) in England is one of the most obvious and one of the largest results of the literary influence of France, but it is not specially due to the romantic school.

The character of that school must be sought much more in its treatment of motives, and particularly in its use of sentiment. It is romantic in its fondness for strange adventures; but this taste is nothing new. The real novelty and the secret of its greatest success was its command of pathos, more especially in the pathetic monologues and dialogues of lovers. It is greatly indebted for this, as has been already remarked, to the Latin poets. The *Aeneid* is turned into a French romance (*Roman d'Eneas*); and the French author of the *Roman de Troie*, who gives the story of the Argonauts in the introductory part of his work, has borrowed much from Ovid's Medea in the *Metamorphoses*. Virgil's Dido and Ovid's Medea had an immense effect on the imagination of the French poets and their followers. From Virgil and Ovid the medieval authors got the suggestion of passionate eloquence, and learned how to manage a love-story in a dramatic way—allowing the characters free scope to express themselves fully. Chivalrous sentiment in the romances is partly due to the example of the Latin authors, who wrote long passionate speeches for their heroines, or letters like that of Phyllis to Demophoon or Ariadne to Theseus and the rest of Ovid's *Heroides*—the source of Chaucer's *Legend of Good Women*. The idea of the lover as the servant of his mistress was also taken first of all from the Latin amatory poets. And the success of the new romantic school was gained by the working together of those ideas and examples, the new creation of chivalrous and courteous love out of those elements.

The ideas are the same in the lyric as in the narrative poetry; and it is allowable to describe a large part of the French romantic poems as being the expression in narrative of the ideas which had been lyrically uttered in the poetry of Provence—

> The love of honour and the honour of love.

The well-known phrase of Sidney is the true rendering of the

Provençal spirit; it is found nearly in the same form in the old language—

> Quar non es joys, si non l'adutz honors,
> Ni es honors, si non l'adutz amors.

(There is no joy, if honour brings it not; nor is there honour if love brings it not.)

The importance of all this for the history of Europe can scarcely be over-estimated. It was the beginning of a classical renaissance through the successful appropriation of classical ideas in modern languages and modern forms. It is true that the medieval version of the *Aeneid* or of the story of the Argonauts may appear exceedingly quaint and 'Gothic' and childish, if it be thought of in comparison with the original; but if it be contrasted with the style of narrative which was in fashion before it, the *Roman d'Eneas* comes out as something new and promising. There is ambition in it, and the ambition is of the same sort as has produced all the finer sentimental fiction since. If it is possible anywhere to trace the pedigree of fashions in literature, it is here. All modern novelists are descended from this French romantic poetry of the twelfth century, and therefore from the classical poets to whom so much of the life of the French romances can be traced. The great poets of the Renaissance carry on in their own way the processes of adaptation which were begun in the twelfth century, and, besides that, many of them are directly indebted—Ariosto and Spenser, for example—to medieval romance.

Further, all the chivalrous ideals of the modern world are derived from the twelfth century. Honour and loyalty would have thriven without the chivalrous poets, as they had thriven before them in every nation on earth. But it is none the less true that the tradition of honour was founded for the sixteenth century and the eighteenth and the present day in Europe by the poets of the twelfth century.

The poetical doctrine of love, which is so great a part of chivalry, has had one effect both on civilization in general and on particular schools of poetry which it is hard to sum up and to understand. It is sometimes a courtly game like that described in the life of the troubadour quoted above; the lady pleased at the honour paid her and ready to accept the poet's worship; the lady's husband either amused by it all, or otherwise, if not amused, at any rate prevented by the rules of polite society from objecting; the poet enamoured according to the same code of law, with as much sincerity as that law and his own disposition might allow; thoroughly occupied with his own craft of verse and with the new illustrations from natural or civil history by means of which he hoped to make a name and go beyond all other poets. The difficulty is to know how much there is of pretence and artifice in the game. It is certain that the Provençal lyric poetry, and the other poetry derived from it in other languages, has many excellences besides the ingenious repetition of stock ideas in cleverly varied patterns of rhyme. The poets are not all alike, and the poems of one poet are not all alike. The same poem of Bernart de Ventadour contains a beautiful, true, fresh description of the sky-lark singing and falling in the middle of the song through pure delight in the rays of the sun; and also later an image of quite a different sort: the lover looking in the eyes of his mistress and seeing himself reflected there is in danger of the same fate as Narcissus, who pined away over his own reflection in the well. Imagination and Fancy are blended and interchanged in the troubadours as much as in any modern poet. But apart from all questions of their value, there is no possible doubt that the Provençal idealism is the source, though not the only source, to which all the noblest lyric poetry of later times and other nations may be referred for its ancestry. The succession of schools (or whatever the right name may be) can be traced with absolute certainty through Dante and Petrarch in the fourteenth century to Ronsard and Spenser in the sixteenth, and further still.

The society which invented good manners and the theory of honour, which is at the beginning of all modern poetry and of all novels as well, is often slighted by modern historians. The vanity, the artifice, the pedantry can easily be noted and dismissed. The genius of the several writers is buried in the difficulty and un-familiarity of the old languages, even where it has not been destroyed and lost in other ways. But still the spirit of Provençal lyric and of old French romance can be proved to be, at the very lowest estimate, the beginning of modern civilization, as distinct from the earlier Middle Ages.

4
The Romances

ALL THROUGH THE TIME between the Norman Conquest and
Chaucer one feels that *the Court* is what determines the character of
poetry and prose. The English writers almost always have to bear in
mind their inferiority to French, and it is possible to describe their
efforts during three centuries (1100–1400) as generally directed
towards the ideal of French poetry, a struggle to realize in English
what had been already achieved in French, to make English literature polite.

In the history of the English romances this may be tested in
various ways. To begin with, there is the fact that many writers
living in England wrote French, and that some French romances,
not among the worst, were composed in England. It can hardly be
doubted that such was the case with the famous love-story of *Amadas
and Ydoine*; it is certain that the romance of *Ipomedon* was composed by an Englishman, Hue de Rotelande. Those two works of
fiction are, if not the noblest, at any rate among the most refined of
their species; *Amadas and Ydoine* is as perfect a romance of true
love as *Amadis of Gaul* in later days—a history which possibly
derived the name of its hero from the earlier Amadas. *Ipomedon* is
equally perfect in another way, being one of the most clever and
successful specimens of the conventionally elegant work which was
practised by imitative poets after the fashion had been established.
There is no better romance to look at in order to see what things
were thought important in the 'school', i.e. among the well-bred
unoriginal writers who had learned the necessary style of verse, and

who could turn out a showy piece of new work by copying the patterns they had before them. Both *Ipomedon* and *Amadas and Ydoine* are in the best possible style—the genteelest of tunes. The fact is clear, that in the twelfth century literary refinement was as possible in England as in France, so long as one used the French language.

It must not be supposed that everything written in French, whether in France or England, was courtly or refined. There is plenty of rough French written in England—some of it very good, too, like the prose story of Fulk Fitzwaryn, which many people would find much more lively than the genteel sentimental novels. But while French could be used for all purposes, polite or rude, English was long compelled to be rude and prevented from competing on equal terms with the language of those 'who have used court'.

It is very interesting to see how the English translated and adapted the polite French poems, because the different examples show so many different degrees of ambition and capacity among the native English. In the style of the English romances—of which there are a great many varieties—one may read the history of the people; the romances bring one into relation with different types of mind and different stages of culture. What happened to *Ipomedon* is a good illustration. First there is the original French poem—a romantic tale in verse written in the regular French short couplets of octosyllabic lines—well and correctly written by a man of English birth. In this production Hue de Rotelande, the author, meant to do his best and to beat all other competitors. He had the right sort of talent for this—not for really original imagination, but for the kind of work that was most in fashion in his time. He did not, like some other poets, look for a subject or a groundwork in a Breton lay, or an Arabian story brought from the East by a traveller; instead of that he had read the most successful romances and he picked out of them, here and there, what suited him best for a new combination. He took, for example, the idea of the lover who falls in love with a lady he has never seen (an idea much older than the French romantic school, but that does not matter, for the present); he took the story of the proud lady won by faithful service; he took from one of the Arthurian romances another device which is older that any particular literature, the champion appearing, disguised in different colours, on three successive days. In *Ipomedon*, of course, the days are days of tournament, and the different disguises three several suits of armour. The scene of the story is Apulia and Calabria, chosen for no particular reason except perhaps to get away from the scene of the British romances. The hero's name, Hippomedon, is Greek, like the names in the *Romance of Thebes*, like Palamon and Arcita, which are taken from the Greek names Palæmon and Archytas. Everything is borrowed, and nothing is used clumsily. *Ipomedon* is made according to a certain prescription, and it is made exactly in the terms of the prescription—a perfect example of the regular fashionable novel, well entitled to its place in any literary museum. This successful piece was turned into English in at least two versions. One of these imitates the original verse of *Ipomedon*, it is written in the ordinary short couplets. In every other respect it fails to represent the original. It leaves things out, and spoils the construction, and misses the point. It is one of our failures. The other version is much more intelligent and careful; the author really was doing as much as he could to render his original truly. But he fails in his choice of verse; he translates the French couplets of *Ipomedon* into a form of stanza, like that which Chaucer burlesques in *Sir Thopas*. It is a very good kind of stanza, and this anonymous English poet manages it well. But it is the wrong sort of measure for that kind of story. It is a dancing, capering measure, and ill suited to translate the French verse, which is quiet, sedate, and not emphatic. These two translations show how the English were apt to fail. Some of them were stupid, and some of them had the wrong sort of skill.

It may be an accident that the English who were so fond of translating from the French should (apparently) have taken so little from the chief French poet of the twelfth century. This was Chrestien de Troyes, who was in his day everything that Racine was five hundred years later; that is to say, he was the successful and accomplished master of all the subtelties of emotion, particularly of love, expressed in the newest, most engaging and captivating style—the perfect manner of good society. His fine narrative poems were thoroughly appreciated in German, where German was at that time the lan-

guage of all the courts, and where the poets of the land were favoured
and protected in the same way as poets in France and Provence. In
English there is only one romance extant which is translated from
Chrestien de Troyes; and the character of the translation is significant: it proves how greatly the circumstances and conditions of
literature in England differed from those of France and Germany.
The romance is *Ywain and Gawain*, a translation of Chrestien's
Yvain, otherwise called *Le Chevalier au Lion*. It is a good romance,
and in style it is much closer to the original than either of the two
versions of *Ipomedon*, lately mentioned; no other of the anonymous
romances comes so near to the standard of Chaucer and Gower. It
is good in manner; its short couplets (in the language of the North
of England) reproduce very well the tone of French narrative verse.
But the English writer is plainly unable to follow the French in all
the effusive passages; he thinks the French is too long, and he cuts
down the speeches. On the other hand (to show the difference
between different countries), the German translator Hartmann von
Aue, dealing with the same French poem, admires the same things
as the French author, and spins out his translation to a greater length
than the original. Another historical fact of the same sort is that the
English seem to have neglected the *Roman d'Eneas*; while German
historians note that it was a translation of this French poem, the
Eneide of Heinrich van Valdeke, which first introduced the
courteous literary form of romance into Germany. German poetry
about the year 1200 was fully the equal of French, in the very
qualities on which the French authors prided themselves. England
was labouring far behind.

It is necessary to judge England in comparison with France, if
the history of medieval poetry is to be written and studied at all.
But the comparison ought not to be pressed so far as to obliterate all
the genuine virtues of the English writers because they are not the
same as the French. There is another consideration also which ought
not to be left out. It is true that the most remarkable thing in
the French romances was their 'language of the heart', their skill
in rendering passion and emotion—their 'sensibility', to use an
eighteenth-century name for the same sort of disposition. But this
emotional skill, this ingenious use of passionate language in

soliloquies and dialogues, was not the only attraction in the French romances. It was the most important thing at the time, and historically it is what gives those romances, of Chrestien de Troyes and others, their rank among the poetical ideas of the world. It was through their sensibility that they enchanted their own time, and this was the spirit which passed on from them to later generations through the prose romances of the fourteenth century, such as *Amadis of Gaul*, to those of the seventeenth century, such as the *Grand Cyrus* or *Cassandra*. To understand what the works of Chrestien de Troyes meant for his contemporaries one cannot do better than read the letters in which Dorothy Osborne speaks of her favourite characters in the later French prose romances, those 'monstrous fictions', as Scott called them, 'which constituted the amusement of the young and the gay in the age of Charles II'. Writing to Sir William Temple she says: 'Almanzor is as fresh in my memory as if I had visited his tomb but yesterday. . . . You will believe I had not been used to great afflictions when I made his story such an one to me as I cried an hour together for him and was so angry with Alcidiana that for my life I could never love her after it.' Almanzor and Alcidiana, and the sorrows that so touched their gentle readers in the age of Louis XIV and Charles II, were the descendants of Chrestien de Troyes in a direct line; they represent what is enduring and inexhaustible in the spirit of the older polite literature in France. Sentiment in modern fiction can be traced back to Chrestien de Troyes. It is a fashion which was established then and has never been extinguished since; if there is to be any history of ideas at all, this is what has to be recorded as the principal influence in French literature in the twelfth century. But it was not everything, and it was not a simple thing. There are many varieties of sentiment, and besides sentiment there are many other interests in the old French romantic literature. The works of Chrestien de Troyes may be taken as examples again. In one, *Cliges*, there are few adventures; in *Perceval* (the story of the Grail), his last poem, the adventures are many and wonderful. In his *Lancelot*, the sentimental interest is managed in accordance with the rules of the Provençal poetry at its most refined and artificial height; but his story of *Enid* is in substance the same as Tennyson's, a romance which does not need (like Chrestien's *Lancelot*) any study of a special code of behaviour to explain the essence of it. The lovers here are husband and wife (quite against the Provençal rules), and the plot is pure comedy, a misunderstanding cleared away by the truth and faithfulness of the heroine.

Further, although it is true that adventure is not the chief interest with Chrestien de Troyes and his followers, it is not true that it is neglected by them; and besides, although they were the most fashionable and most famous and successful authors of romance, they were not the only story-tellers nor was their method the only one available. There was a form of short story, commonly called *lai* and associated with Brittany, in which there was room for the same kind of matter as in many of the larger romances, but not for the same expression and effusion of sentiment. The best known are those of Marie de France, who dedicated her book of stories to King Henry of England (Henry II). One of the best of the English short romances, *Sir Launfal*, is taken from Marie de France; her stories have a beauty which was not at the time so enthralling as the charm of the longer stories, and which had nothing like the same influence on the literature of the future, but which now, for those who care to look at it, has much more freshness, partly because it is nearer to the fairy mythology of popular tradition. The longer romances are really modern novels—studies of contemporary life, characters and emotions, mixed up with adventures more or less surprising. The shorter *lais* (like that of *Sir Launfal*) might be compared to the stories of Hans Christian Andersen; they are made in the same way. Like many of Andersen's tales, they are borrowed from folk-lore; like them, again, they are not mere transcripts from an uneducated story-teller. They are 'old wives' tales', but they are put into fresh literary form. This new form may occasionally interfere with something in the original traditional version, but it does not, either with Marie de France or with Andersen, add too much to the original. Curiously, there is an example in English, among the shorter rhyming romances, of a story which Andersen has told in his own way under the title of the *Travelling Companion*. The English *Sir Amadace* is unfortunately not one of the best of the short stories—not nearly as good as *Sir Launfal*—but still it shows how a common folk-lore plot, the story of the Grateful Dead, might be turned into literary form without losing all its original force and without being transformed into a mere vehicle for modern literary ambitions.

The relations between folk-lore and literature are forced on the attention when one is studying the Middle Ages, and perhaps most of all in dealing with this present subject, the romances of the age of chivalry. In Anglo-Saxon literature it is much less to the fore, probably not because there was little of it really, but because so little has been preserved. In the eleventh and twelfth centuries there was a great stirring-up of popular mythology in a number of countries, so that it came to be noticed, and passed into scores of books, both in the form of plots for stories, and also in scientific remarks made by investigators and historians. Giraldus Cambrensis is full of folk-lore, and about the same time Walter Map (in his *De Nugis Curialium*) and Gervase of Tilbury (in his *Otia Imperialia*) were taking notes of the same sort. Both Giraldus and Walter Map were at home in Wales, and it was particularly in the relation between the Welsh and their neighbours that the study of folk-lore was encouraged; both the historical study, as in the works of these Latin authors just named, and the traffic in stories to be used for literary purposes in the vernacular languages whether French or English.

The 'matter of Britain' in the stories of Tristram, Gawain, Perceval and Lancelot came to be associated peculiarly with the courteous sentimental type of romance which had such vogue and such influence in the Middle Ages. But the value of this 'matter'—the Celtic stories—was by no means exclusively connected with the ambitious literary art of Chrestien and others like him. Apart from form altogether, it counts for something that such a profusion of stories was sent abroad over all the nations. They were interesting and amusing, in whatever language they were told. They quickened up people's imaginations and gave them something to think about, in the same way as the Italian novels which were so much read in the time of Shakespeare, or the trashy German novels in the time of Shelley.

It is much debated among historians whether it was from Wales or Brittany that these stories passed into general circulation. It seems most probable that the two Welsh countries on both sides of the

Channel gave stories to their neighbours—to the Normans both in
France and England, and to the English besides on the Welsh
borders. It seems most probable at any rate that the French had not
to wait for the Norman Conquest before they picked up any Celtic
stories. The Arthurian names in Italy (mentioned already above,
p. 38) are found too early, and the dates do not allow time for the
stories to make their way, and find favour, and tempt people in
Lombardy to call their children after Gawain instead of a patron
saint. It is certain that both in Brittany—Little Britain—and in
Wales King Arthur was a hero, whose return was to put all things
right. It was to fulfil this prophecy that Geoffrey Plantagenet's son
was called Arthur, and a Provençal poet hails the child with these
auspices: 'Now the Bretons have got their Arthur.' Other writers
speak commonly of the 'Breton folly'—this hope of a deliverer was
the Breton vanity, well known and laughed at by the more practical
people across the border. WHAT??

Arthur, however, was not the proper hero of the romantic tales,
either in their shorter, more popular form or in the elaborate work
of the courtly school. In many of the *lais* he is never mentioned; in
most of the romances, long or short, early or late, he has nothing to
do except to preside over the feast, at Christmas or Whitsuntide, and
wait for adventures. So he is represented in the English poem of
Sir Gawayn and the Grene Knyght. The stories are told not about
King Arthur, but about Gawain or Perceval, Lancelot or Pelleas or
Pellenore.

The great exception to this general rule is the history of Arthur
which was written by Geoffrey of Monmouth in the first half of the
twelfth century as part of his Latin history of Britain. This history
of Arthur was of course translated wherever Geoffrey was translated,
and sometimes it was picked out for separate treatment, as by the
remarkable author of the *Morte Arthure*, one of the best of the
alliterative poems. Arthur had long been known in Britain as a great
leader against the Saxon invaders; Geoffrey of Monmouth took up
and developed this idea in his own way, making Arthur a successful
opponent not of the Saxons merely but of Rome; a conqueror of
kingdoms, himself an emperor before whom the power of Rome was
humbled. In consequence of which the 'Saxons' came to think of

their country as Britain, and to make Arthur their national hero, in the same way as Charlemagne was the national hero in France. Arthur also, like Charlemagne, came to be generally respected all over Christendom, in Norway and Iceland, as well as Italy and Greece. Speaking generally, whenever Arthur is a great conquering hero like Alexander or Charlemagne this idea of him is due to Geoffrey of Monmouth; the stories where he only appears as holding a court and sending out champions are stories that have come from popular tradition, or are imitations of such stories. But there are some exceptions. For one thing, Geoffrey's representation of Arthur is not merely a composition after the model of Alexander the Great or Charlemagne; the story of Arthur's fall at the hands of his nephew is traditional. And when Layamon a 'Saxon' turned the French rhyming version of Geoffrey into English—Layamon's *Brut* —he added a number of things which are neither in the Latin nor the French, but obtained by Layamon himself independently, some-how or other, from the Welsh. Layamon lived on the banks of the Severn, and very probably he may have done the same kind of note-taking in Wales or among Welsh acquaintances as was done by Walter Map a little earlier. Layamon's additions are of great worth; he tells the story of the passing of Arthur, and it is from Layamon, ultimately, that all the later versions—Malory's and Tennyson's—are derived.

None of the English authors can compete with the French poets as elegant writers dealing with contemporary manners. But apart from that kind of work almost every variety of interest may be found in the English stories. There are two, *King Horn* and *Havelok the Dane*, which appear to be founded on national English traditions coming down from the time of the Danish wars. *King Horn* is remarkable for its metre—short rhyming couplets, but not in the regular eight-syllable lines which were imitated from the French. The verse appears to be an adaptation of the old native English measure, fitted with regular rhymes. Rhyme was used in continental German poetry, and in Icelandic, and occasionally in Anglo-Saxon, before there were any French examples to follow; and *King Horn* is one thing surviving to show how the English story-tellers might have got on if they had not paid so much attention to the French authorities in rhyme. The story of Havelok belongs to the town of Grimsby particularly and to the Danelaw, the district of England occupied by Danish settlers. The name Havelok is the Danish, or rather the Norwegian, Anlaf or Olaf, and the story seems to be a tradition in which two historical Olafs have been confused—one the Olaf who was defeated at the battle of Brunanburh, the other the Olaf who won the battle of Maldon—Olaf Tryggvason, King of Norway. *Havelok*, the English story, is worth reading as a good specimen of popular English poetry in the thirteenth century, a story where the subject and the scene are English, where the manners are not too fine, and where the hero, a king's son disinherited and un-recognized, lives as a servant for a long time and so gives the author a chance of describing common life and uncourtly manners. And he does this very well, particularly in the athletic sports where Havelok distinguishes himself—an excellent piece to compare with the funeral games which used to be a necessary part of every regular epic poem. *Horn* and *Havelok*, though they belong to England, are scarcely to be reckoned as part of the 'matter of Britain', at least as that was understood by the French author who used the term. There are other stories which will not go easily into that or into either of the two other divisions. One of these is the story of *Floris and Blanche-fleur*, which was turned into English in the thirteenth century—one of the oldest among the rhyming romances. This is one of the many stories that came from the East. It is the history of two young lovers who are separated for a time—a very well known and favourite type of story. This is the regular plot in the Greek prose romances, such as that of Heliodorus which was so much admired after the Renaissance. This story of *Floris and Blanchefleur*, however, does not come from Greece, but from the same source as the *Arabian Nights*. Those famous stories, the Thousand and One Nights, were not known in Europe till the beginning of the eighteenth century, but many things of the same sort had made their way in the Middle Ages into France, and this was the best of them all. It is found in German and Dutch, as well as in English; also in Swedish and Danish, in the same kind of short couplets—showing how widely the fashions of literature were prescribed by France among all the Teutonic races.

M E L—C

How various the styles of romance might be is shown by two poems which are both found in the famous *Auchinleck* manuscript in Edinburgh, *Sir Orfeo* and *Sir Tristrem*. The stories are two of the best known in the world. *Sir Orfeo* is Orpheus. But this version of Orpheus and Eurydice is not a translation from anything classical; it is far further from any classical original than even the very free and distinctly 'Gothic' rendering of Jason and Medea at the beginning of the old French tale of Troy. The story of Orpheus has passed through popular tradition before it turns into *Sir Orfeo*. It shows how readily folk-lore will take a suggestion from book-learning, and how easily it will make a classical fable into the likeness of a Breton lay. Orfeo was a king, and also a good harper:

> He hath a queen full fair of price
> That is clepèd Dame Erodys.

One day in May Queen Erodys slept in her orchard, and when she awoke was overcome with affliction because of a dream—a king had appeared to her, with a thousand knights and fifty ladies, riding on snow-white steeds.

> The king had a crown on his head
> It was no silver, ne gold red,
> All it was of precious stone,
> As bright as sun forsooth it shone.

He made her ride on a white palfrey to his own land, and showed her castles and towers, meadows, fields and forests; then he brought her home, and told her that the next day she would be taken away for ever.

The king kept watch on the morrow with two hundred knights; but there was no help; among them all she was fetched away 'with the faerie'. Then King Orfeo left his kingdom, and went out to the wilderness to the 'holtes hoar' barefoot, taking nothing of all his wealth but his harp only.

> In summer he liveth by hawès
> That on hawthorne groweth by shawès,
> And in winter by root and rind
> For other thing may he none find.

No man could tell of his sore
That he suffered ten year and more,
He that had castle and tower,
Forest, frith, both field and flower,
Now hath he nothing that him liketh
But wild beasts that by him striketh.

Beasts and birds came to listen to his harping—

When the weather is clear and bright,
He taketh his harp anon right;
Into the wood it ringeth shrill
As he could harpè at his will:
The wildè bestès that there beth
For joy about him they geth
All the fowlès that there were
They comen about him there
To hear harping that was fine
So mickle joy was therein.

· · · ·

Oft he saw him beside
In the hotè summer tide
The king of Fayré with his rout
Came to hunt all about.

· · · ·

Sometimes he saw the armed host of the Faerie; sometimes knights
and ladies together, in bright attire, riding an easy pace, and along
with them all manner of minstrelsy. One day he followed a company
of the Fairy ladies as they were hawking by the river (or rather the
rivere—i.e. the bank of the stream) at

Pheasant heron and cormorant;
The fowls out of the river flew
Every falcon his game slew.

King Orfeo saw that and laughed and rose up from his resting-place
and followed, and found his wife among them; but neither might
speak with the other—

But there might none with other speak
Though she him knew and he her, eke.

But he took up his harp and followed them fast, over stock and stone, and when they rode into a hillside—'in at the roche'—he went in after them.

> When he was into the roche y-go
> Well three mile, and some deal mo
> He came to a fair countray
> Was as bright as any day.

There in the middle of a lawn he saw a fair high castle of gold and silver and precious stones.

> No man might tell ne think in thought
> The riches that therein was wrought.

The porter let him in, as a minstrel, and he was brought before the king and queen. 'How do you come here?' said the king; 'I never sent for you, and never before have I known a man so hardy as to come unbidden.' Then Sir Orfeo put in a word for the minstrels; 'It is our manner', he said, 'to come to every man's house unbidden',

> 'And though we nought welcome be
> Yet we must proffer our game or glee.'

Then he took his harp and played, and the king offered him whatever he should ask.

> 'Minstrel, me liketh well thy glee.'

Orfeo asked for the lady bright. 'Nay', said the king, 'that were a foul match, for in her there is no blemish and thou art rough and black'. 'Fouler still', said Orfeo, 'to hear a leasing from a king's mouth'; and the king then let him go with good wishes, and Orfeo and Erodys went home. The steward had kept the kingdom truly; 'thus came they out of care'.

It is all as simple as can be; a rescue out of fairyland, through the power of music; the ideas are found everywhere, in ballads and stories. The ending is happy, and nothing is said of the injunction not to look back. It was probably left out when Orpheus was turned into a fairy tale, on account of the power of music; the heart of the people felt that Orpheus the good harper ought not to be subjected to the common plot. For there is nothing commoner in romance or

in popular tales than forgetfulness like that of Orpheus when he lost
Eurydice; the plot of *Sir Launfal* e.g. turns on that; he was warned
not to speak of his fairy wife, but he was led, by circumstances over
which he had no control, to boast of her—

> To speke ne mightè he forgo
> And said the queen before:
> 'I have lovèd a fairer woman
> Than thou ever laidest thine eye upon,
> This seven year and more!'

The drama of *Lohengrin* keeps this idea before the public (not to
speak of the opera of *Orfeo*), and *Lohengrin* is a medieval German
romance. The Breton lay of Orpheus would not have been in any
way exceptional if it had kept to the original fable; the beauty of it
loses nothing by the course which it has preferred to take, the happy
ending. One may refer to it as a standard, to show what can be done
in the medieval art of narrative, with the simplest elements and
smallest amount of decoration. It is minstrel poetry, popular poetry
—the point is clear when King Orfeo excuses himself to the King of
Faerie by the rules of his profession as a minstrel; that was intended
to produce a smile, and applause perhaps, among the audience. But
though a minstrel's poem it is far from rude, and it is quite free from
the ordinary faults of rambling and prosing, such as Chaucer
ridiculed in his *Geste of Sir Thopas*. It is all in good compass, and
coherent; nothing in it is meaningless or ill-placed.

Sir Tristrem is a great contrast to *Sir Orfeo*; not an absolute
contrast, for neither is this story rambling or out of compass. The
difference between the two is that *Sir Orfeo* is nearly perfect as an
English representative of the 'Breton lay'—i.e. the short French
romantic story like the *Lais* of Marie de France; while *Sir Tristrem*
represents no French style of narrative poetry, and is not very
successful (though technically very interesting) as an original English
experiment in poetical form. It is distinctly clever, as it is likewise
ambitious. The poet intends to do finer things than the common.
He adopts a peculiar stanza, not one of the easiest—a stanza more
fitted for lyric than narrative poetry, and which is actually used for
lyrical verse by the poet Laurence Minot. It is in short lines, well

managed and effective in their way, but it is a thin tinkling music
to accompany the tragic story.

> Ysonde bright of hewe
>   Is far out in the sea;
> A wind again them blew
>   That sail no might there be;
> So rew the knightes trewe,
>   Tristrem, so rew he,
> Ever as they came newe
>   He one again them three
> Great swink—
>   Sweet Ysonde the free
> Asked Brengwain a drink.
>
> The cup was richly wrought,
>   Of gold it was, the pin;
> In all the world was nought
>   Such drink as there was in;
> Brengwain was wrong bethought
>   To that drink she gan win
> And sweet Ysonde it betaught;
>   She bad Tristrem begin
> To say:
>   Their love might no man twin
> Till their ending day.

The stage is that of a little neat puppet-show; with figures like
those of a miniature, dressed in bright armour, or in scarlet and vair
and grey—the rich cloth, the precious furs, grey and ermine, which
so often represent the glory of this world in the old romances—

> Ysonde of highe pris,
>   The maiden bright of hewe,
> That wered fow and gris
>   And scarlet that was newe;
> In warld was none so wis
>   Of crafte that men knewe.

There is a large group of rhyming romances which might be
named after Chaucer's *Sir Thopas*—the companions of *Sir Thopas*.

Chaucer's burlesque is easily misunderstood. It is criticism, and it is
ridicule; it shows up the true character of the common minstrelsy;
the rambling narrative, the conventional stopgaps, the complacent
childish vanity of the popular artist who has his audience in front
of him and knows all the easy tricks by which he can hold their
attention. Chaucer's *Rime of Sir Thopas* is interrupted by the voice
of common sense—rudely—

> This may well be rime doggerel, quoth he.

But Chaucer has made a good thing out of the rhyme doggerel, and
expresses the pleasant old-fashioned quality of the minstrels'
romances, as well as their absurdities.

His parody touches on the want of plan and method and meaning
in the popular rhymes of chivalry; it is also intended as criticism of
their verse. That verse, of which there are several varieties—there is
more than one type of stanza in *Sir Thopas*—is technically called
rime couée or 'tail-rhyme', and like all patterns of verse it imposes a
certain condition of mind, for the time, on the poets who use it. It
is not absolutely simple, and so it is apt to make the writer well
pleased with himself when he finds it going well; it very readily
becomes monotonous and flat—

> Now cometh the emperour of price,
> Again him rode the king of Galice
>   With full mickle pride;
> The child was worthy under weed
> And sat upon a noble steed
>   By his father side;
> And when he met the emperour
> He valed his hood with great honour
>   And kissed him in that tide;
> And other lords of great valour
> They also kissèd Segramour
>   In heart is not to hide.   (*Emaré.*)

For that reason, because of the monotonous beat of the tail-rhymes
in the middle and at the end of the stanza, it is chosen by the
parodists of Wordsworth in the *Rejected Addresses* when they are
aiming at what they think is flat and insipid in his poetry. But it is

a form of stanza which may be so used as to escape the besetting faults; the fact that it has survived through all the changes of literary fashion, and has been used by poets in all the different centuries, is something to the credit of the minstrels, as against the rude common-sense criticism of the Host of the Tabard when he stopped the *Rime of Sir Thopas*.

Chaucer's catalogue of romances is well known—

> Men speken of romances of prys
> Of Horn Child and of Ypotys
> Of Bevis and Sir Gy,
> Of Sir Libeux and Pleyndamour,
> But Sir Thopas he bereth the flour
> Of royal chivalry.

In this summary, the name of *Pleyndamour* is still a difficulty for historians; it is not known to what book Chaucer is referring. *Ypotis* is curiously placed, for the poem of *Ypotis* is not what is usually reckoned a romance. 'Ypotis' is Epictetus the Stoic philosopher, and the poem is derived from the old moralizing dialogue literature; it is related to the Anglo-Saxon dialogue of Solomon and Saturn. The other four are well known. *Horn Childe* is a later version, in stanzas, of the story of *King Horn*. Bevis of Southampton and Guy of Warwick are among the most renowned, and most popular, of all the chivalrous heroes. In later prose adaptations they were current down to modern times; they were part of the favourite reading of Bunyan, and gave him ideas for the *Pilgrim's Progress*. *Guy of Warwick* was rewritten many times— Chaucer's pupil, Lydgate, took it up and made a new version of it. There was a moral and religious strain in it, which appealed to the tastes of many; the remarkable didactic prose romance of *Tirant the White*, written in Spain in the fifteenth century, is connected with *Guy of Warwick*. Sir Bevis is more ordinary and has no particular moral; it is worth reading, if any one wishes to know what was regularly expected in romances by the people who read, or rather who listened to them. The disinherited hero, the beautiful Paynim princess, the good horse Arundel, the giant Ascapart—these and many other incidents may be paralleled in other stories; the history of Sir Bevis has brought them all together, and all the popular novelist's machinery might be fairly catalogued out of this work alone.

Sir Libeaus—Le Beau Desconnu, the Fair Knight unknown—is a different thing. This also belongs to the School of Sir Thopas—it is minstrels' work, and does not pretend to be anything else. But it is well done. The verse, which is in short measure like that of *Sir Tristrem*, but not in so ambitious a stanza, is well managed—

> That maide knelde in halle
> Before the knightes alle
>   And seide: My lord Arthour!
> A cas ther is befalle
> Worse withinne walle
>   Was never non of dolour.
> My lady of Sinadoune
> Is brought in strong prisoun
>   That was of great valour;
> Sche praith the sende her a knight
> With herte good and light
>   To winne her with honour.

This quotation came from the beginning of the story, and it gives the one problem which has to be solved by the hero. Instead of the mixed adventures of Sir Bevis, there is only one principal one, which gives occasion to all the adventures by the way. The lady of Sinodoun has fallen into the power of two enchanters, and her damsel (with her dwarf attendant) comes to the court of King Arthur to ask for a champion to rescue her. It is a story like that of the Red Cross Knight and Una. If Sir Bevis corresponds to what one may call the ordinary matter of Spenser's *Faerie Queen*, the wanderings, the separations, the dangerous encounters, *Sir Libeaus* resembles those parts of Spenser's story where the plot is most coherent. One of the most beautiful passages in all his work, Britomart in the house of the enchanter Busirane, may have been suggested by *Sir Libeaus*. *Sir Libeaus* is one example of a kind of medieval story, not the greatest, but still good and sound; the Arthurian romance in which Arthur has nothing to do except to preside at the beginning, and afterwards to receive the conquered opponents whom the hero

sends home from successive stages in his progress, to make sub-
mission to the king. Sir Libeaus (his real name is Guinglain, the
son of Gawain) sets out on his journey with the damsel and the
dwarf; at first he is scorned by her, like Sir Gareth of Orkney in
another story of the same sort, but very soon he shows what he can
do at the passage of the Pont Perilous, and in the challenging of the
gerfalcon, and many other trials. Like other heroes of romance, he
falls under the spell of a sorceress who dazzles him with 'fantasm
and faerie', but he escapes after a long delay, and defeats the
magicians of Sinodoun and rescues the lady with a kiss from her
serpent shape which the enchanters have put upon her. Compared
with Spenser's house of Busirane, the scene of Sir Libeaus at
Sinodoun is a small thing. But one does not feel as in *Sir Tristrem*
the discrepancy between the miniature stage, the small bright figures,
and the tragic meaning of their story. Here the story is not tragic;
it is a story that the actors understand and can play rightly. There
are no characters and no motives beyond the scope of a fairy tale—

> Sir Libeaus, knight corteis
> Rode into the paleis
>   And at the halle alighte;
> Trompes, hornes, schalmeis,
> Before the highe dais,
>   He herd and saw with sight;
> Amid the halle floor
> A fire stark and store
>   Was light and brende bright;
> Then farther in he yede
> And took with him his steed
>   That halp him in the fight.
>
> Libeaus inner gan pace
> To behold each place,
>   The hales in the halle;   *niches*
> Of main more ne lasse
> Ne saw he body ne face
>   But menstrales clothed in palle;
> With harpe, fithele and rote,
> And with organes note,

> Great glee they maden alle,
> With citole and sautrie,
> So moche menstralsie
> Was never withinne walle.

As if to show the range and the difference of style in English romance, there is another story written like *Sir Libeaus* in the reign of Edward III, taken from the same Arthurian legend and beginning in the same way, which has scarcely anything in common with it except the general resemblance in the plot. This is *Sir Gawain and the Green Knight*, one of the most original works in medieval romance. It is written in alliterative blank verse, divided into irregular periods which have rhyming tailpieces at the end of them—

> As hit is stad and stoken
> In story stif and stronge
> With leal letters loken
> In land so has been longe.

While the story of *Sir Libeaus* is found in different languages—French, Italian, German—there is no other extant older version of *Gawain and the Green Knight*. But the separate incidents are found elsewhere, and the scene to begin with is the usual one: Arthur at his court, Arthur keeping high festival and waiting for 'some main marvel'. The adventure comes when it is wanted; the Green Knight on his green horse rides into the king's hall—half-ogre, by the look of him, to challenge the Round Table. What he offers is a 'jeopardy', a hazard, a wager. 'Will any gentleman cut off my head', says he, 'on condition that I may have a fair blow at him, and no favour, in a twelvemonth's time? Or if you would rather have it so, let me have the first stroke, and I promise to offer my neck in turn, when a year has gone.' This is the beheading game which is spoken of in other stories (one of them an old Irish comic romance) but which seems to have been new at that time to the knights of King Arthur. It is rightly considered dangerous; and so it proved when Sir Gawain had accepted the jeopardy. For after Gawain had cut off the stranger's head, the Green Knight picked it up by the hair, and held it up, and it spoke and summoned Gawain to meet him at the Green Chapel in a year's space, and bide the return blow.

This is more surprising than anything in *Sir Bevis* or *Sir Guy*. Not much is done by the writer to explain it; at the same time nothing is left vague. The author might almost have been a modern novelist with a contempt for romance, trying, by way of experiment, to work out a 'supernatural' plot with the full strength of his reason; merely accepting the fabulous story, and trying how it will go with accessories from real life, and with modern manners and conversation. There is none of the minstrel's cant in this work, none of the cheap sensations, the hackneyed wonders such as are ridiculed in *Sir Thopas*. Only, the incident on which the whole story turns, the device of the beheading game, is a piece of traditional romance. It is not found in every language, but it is fairly well known. It is not as common as the lady turned into a serpent, or the man into a werewolf, but still it is not invented, it is borrowed by the English poet, and borrowed for a work which always, even in the beheading scenes, is founded on reality.

It is probable that the author of *Sir Gawain* is also the author of three other poems (not romances) which are found along with it in the same manuscript—the *Pearl*, *Cleanness*, and *Patience*. He is a writer with a gift for teaching, of a peculiar sort. He is not an original philosopher, and his reading appears to have been the usual sort of thing among fairly educated men. He does not try to get away from the regular authorities, and he is not afraid of commonplaces. But he has great force of will, and a strong sense of the difficulties of life; also high spirits and great keenness. His memory is well supplied from all that he has gone through. The three sporting episodes in *Sir Gawain*, the deer-hunt (in Christmas week, killing the hinds), the boar-hunt and the fox-hunt, are not only beyond question as to their scientific truth; the details are remembered without study because the author has lived in them, and thus, minute as they are, they are not wearisome. They do not come from a careful notebook; they are not like the descriptions of rooms and furniture in painstaking novels. The landscapes and the weather of *Sir Gawain* are put in with the same freedom. The author has a talent especially for winter scenes. 'Grim Nature's visage hoar' had plainly impressed his mind, and not in a repulsive way. The winter 'mist hackles' (copes of mist) on the hills, the icicles on the stones, the swollen streams, all come into his work—a relief from the too ready illustrations of spring and summer which are scattered about in medieval stories.

The meaning of the story is in the character of Gawain. Like some other romances, this is a chivalrous *Pilgrim's Progress*. Gawain, so much vilified by authors who should have known better, is for this poet, as he is for Chaucer, the perfection of courtesy. He is also the servant of Our Lady, and bears her picture on his shield, along with the pentangle which is the emblem of her Five Joys, as well as the Five Wounds of Christ. The poem is the ordeal of Gawain; Gawain is tried in courage and loyalty by his compact with the Green Knight; he is tried in loyalty and temperance when he is wooed by the wanton conversation of the lady in the castle. The author's choice of a plot is justified, because what he wants is an ordeal of courage, and that is afforded by the Green Knight's 'jeopardy'.

The alliterative poetry is almost always stronger than the tales in rhyme, written with more zest, not so much in danger of droning and sleepiness as the school of Sir Thopas undoubtedly is. But there is a great difference among the alliterative romances. *William of Palerne*, for example, is vigorous, but to little purpose, because the author has not understood the character of the French poem which he has translated, and has misapplied his vigorous style to the handling of a rather sophisticated story which wanted the smooth, even, unemphatic, French style to express it properly. *The Wars of Alexander* is the least distinguished of the group; there was another alliterative story of Alexander, of which only fragments remain. The *Chevelere Assigne*, the 'Knight of the Swan', is historically interesting, as giving the romantic origin of Godfrey the Crusader, who is the last of the Nine Worthies. Though purely romantic in its contents, the *Chevalier au Cygne* belongs to one of the French narrative groups usually called epic—the epic of *Antioch*, which is concerned with the first Crusade. The *Gest historial of the Destruction of Troy* is of great interest; it is the liveliest of all the extant 'Troy Books', and it has all the good qualities of the fourteenth-century alliterative school, without the exaggeration and violence which was the common fault of this style, as the contrary fault of tameness was the danger of the rhyming romances. But the alliterative poem which ranks along with *Sir Gawayne* as an original work with a distinct and fresh comprehension of its subject is the *Morte Arthure*. This has some claim to be called an epic poem, an epic of the modern kind, composed with a definite theory. The author takes the heroic view of Arthur given by Geoffrey of Monmouth, and turns his warfare into a reflection of the glory of King Edward III; not casually, but following definite lines, with almost as much tenacity as the author of *Sir Gawayne*, and, of course, with a greater theme. The tragedy of Arthur in Malory to some extent repeats the work of this poet— whose name was Huchoun of the Awle Ryale; it may have been Sir Hugh of Eglinton.

5
Songs and Ballads

KING CANUTE'S BOAT-SONG has some claim to be the earliest
English song in rhyme—

> Merie sungen the muneches binnen Ely
> Tha Knut king rew therby:
> Roweth, knihtes, ner the land
> And here we thes muneches sang.

If this claim be disallowed, then the first is St. Godric, the hermit of
Finchale in the reign of Henry II—his hymn to Our Lady and the
hymn to St. Nicholas. These are preserved along with the music
(like the Cuckoo song which comes later); the manuscript of the
poems of Godric is copied in the frontispiece to Saintsbury's *History
of English Prosody*; it proves many interesting things. It is obvious
that musical notation is well established; and it seems to follow that
with a good musical tradition there may be encouragement for lyric
poetry apart from any such 'courtly' circumstances as have been
described in another chapter. There is no doubt about this. While it
is certain on the one hand that the lyrical art of the Middle Ages was
carried furthest in courtly society by the French, Provençal, German
and Italian poets, it is equally certain that the art of music flourished
also in out-of-the-way places. And as in those days musical and
poetical measures, tunes and words, generally went together, the
development of music would mean the development of poetical
forms, of lyric stanzas. Music flourished in England most of all in
Godric's country, the old Northumbria. Giraldus Cambrensis, who

has been quoted already for his story of the wake and the English love-song, gives in another place a remarkable description of the part-singing which in his time was cultivated where it is most in favour at the present day—in Wales, and in England north of the Humber. Where people met to sing in parts, where music, therefore, was accurate and well studied, there must have been careful patterns of stanza. Not much remains from a date so early as this, nor even for a century after the time of Godric and Giraldus. But towards the end of the reign of Edward I lyric poems are found more frequently, often careful in form. And in judging of their art it is well to remember that it is not necessary to refer them to the courtly schools for their origin. Country people might be good judges of lyric; they might be as exacting in their musical and poetical criticisms as any persons of quality could be. Hence while it is certain that England before the time of Chaucer was generally rustic and provincial in its literary taste, it does not follow that the rustic taste was uninstructed or that the art was poor. The beauty of the English songs between 1300 and 1500 is not that of the nobler lyric as it was (for example) practised and described by Dante. But the beauty is undeniable, and it is the beauty of an art which has laws of its own; it is poetry, not the primitive elements of poetry. In art, it is not very far from that of the earlier Provençal poets. For everywhere, it should be remembered, the noble lyric poetry was ready to draw from the popular sources, to adapt and imitate the rustic themes; as on the other hand the common people were often willing to take up the courtly forms.

The earliest rhyming songs are more interesting from their associations than their own merits; though Canute and St. Godric are certainly able to put a good deal of meaning into few words. Godric's address to St. Nicholas is particularly memorable for its bearing on his own history. Godric had been a sea captain in his youth (like another famous author of hymns, the Rev. John Newton) and St. Nicholas is the patron saint of sailors. Godric, whose operations were in the Levant, had often prayed to St. Nicholas of Bari, and he brings the name of the saint's own city into his hymn, by means of a sacred pun. 'Saint Nicholas', he says, 'build us a far sheen house—

At thi burch at thi bare
Sainte Nicholaes bring us wel thare.'

'Bare' here means shrine, literally, but Godric is thinking also of the name of the 'burgh', the city of Bari to which the relics of the saint had been lately brought.

Religious lyric poetry is not separate from other kinds, and it frequently imitates the forms and language of worldly songs. The *Luve Ron* of the Friar Minor Thomas de Hales is one of the earliest poems of a type something between the song and the moral poem—a lyric rather far away from the music of a song, more like the lyrics of modern poets, meant to be read rather than sung, yet keeping the lyrical stave. One passage in it is on the favourite theme of the 'snows of yester year'—

> Where is Paris and Heleyne
> That were so bright and fair of blee!

This is earlier in date than the famous collection in the Harleian MS., which is everything best worth remembering in the old lyrical poetry—

> Betwene Mersche and Averil
> When spray beginneth to springe.

The lyrical contents of this book (there are other things besides the songs—a copy of *King Horn*, e.g.)—the songs of this Harleian MS. —are classified as religious, amatory and satirical; but a better division is simply into songs of love and songs of scorn. The division is as old and as constant as anything in the world, and the distinction between 'courtly' and 'popular' does not affect it. In the older court poetry of Iceland, as in the later of Provence and Germany, the lyric of scorn and the lyric of praise were equally recognized. The name 'Wormtongue' given to an Icelandic poet for his attacking poems would do very well for many of the Provençals—for Sordello, particularly, whose best-known poem is his lyrical satire on the Kings of Christendom. It depends, of course, on fashion how the lyrical attack shall be developed. In England it could not be as subtle as in the countries of Bertran de Born or Walter von der Vogelweide, where the poet was a friend and enemy of some among the greatest of the earth. The political songs in the Harleian manuscript are anonymous, and express the heart of the people. The earliest in date and the best known is the song of Lewes—a blast of laughter from the partisans of Simon de Montfort following up the pursuit of their defeated adversaries—thoroughly happy and contemptuous, and not cruel. It is addressed to 'Richard of Almain', Richard the king's brother, who was looked on as the bad counsellor of his nephew Edward—

> Sir Simon de Montfort hath swore by his chin,
> Hadde he now here the Erl of Warin
> Sholde he never more come to his inn
> With shelde, ne with spere, ne with other gin
>   To helpe of Windesore!
> *Richard! thah thou be ever trichard,*
> *Trichen shalt thou never more!*

This very spirited song is preserved together with some others dealing with later events in the life of Edward. One of them is a long poem of exultation over the death of the King's Scottish rebels, Sir William Wallace and Sir Simon Fraser; the author takes great pleasure in the treatment of Wallace by the King and the hangman—

> Sir Edward oure King, that full is of pité
> The Waleis' quarters sende to his owne countré
> On four half to honge, here mirour to be
> Ther upon to thenche, that monie mihten see
>   And drede:
>   Why nolden hie be war,
>   Of the bataile of Donbar
>   How evele hem con spede?

The same poet gibes at a Scottish rebel who was then still living and calls him a 'king of summer' and 'King Hob'—

> Nou kyng Hobbe in the mures gongeth.

This King Hob of the moors was Robert the Bruce, wandering, as Barbour describes him, over the land. There is another very vigorous and rather long piece on a recent defeat of the French by the Flemings at Courtrai—

> The Frenshe came to Flaundres so light so the hare
> Er hit were midnight, hit fell hem to care
> Hie were caught by the net, so bird is in snare
> With rouncin and with stede:
> The Flemishe hem dabbeth on the hed bare,
> Hie nolden take for hem raunsoun ne ware
> Hie doddeth off here hevedes, fare so hit fare,
> And thare to haveth hie nede.

This style of political journalism in rhyme was carried on later with much spirit, and one author is well known by name and has had his poems often edited—Lawrence Minot, a good workman who is sometimes undervalued. Lawrence Minot has command of various lyrical measures; he has the clear sharp phrasing which belongs generally to his northern dialect, and he can put contempt into his voice with no recourse to bad language. After describing the threats and boasting of the French, when Minot remarks

> And yet is England as it was,

the effect is just where it ought to be, between wind and water; the enemy is done for. It is like Prior's observation to Boileau, in the *Ode* on the taking of Namur, and the surrender of the French garrison—

> Each was a Hercules, you tell us,
> Yet out they marched like common men.

Besides the songs of attack, there are also comic poems, simply amusing without malice—such is the excellent Harleian piece on the *Man in the Moon*, which is the meditation of a solitary reveller, apparently thinking out the problem of the Man and his thorn-bush and offering sympathy: 'Did you cut a bundle of thorns, and did the heyward come and make you pay? Ask him to drink, and we will get your pledge redeemed'.

> If thy wed is y-take, bring home the truss;
> Set forth thine other foot, stride over sty!
> We shall pray the heyward home to our house,
> And maken him at ease, for the maistry!
> Drink to him dearly of full good bouse,
> And our dame Douce shall sitten him by;

> When that he is drunk as a dreynt mouse
> Then we shall borrow the wed at the bailie!

A Franciscan brother in Ireland, Friar Michael of Kildare, composed some good nonsensical poems—one of them a rigmarole in which part of the joke is the way he pretends to rhyme and then sticks in a word that does not rhyme, asking all through for admiration of his skill in verse. As a poetical joke it is curious, and shows that Brother Michael was a critic and knew the terms of his art. There are many literary games in the Middle Ages, nonsense rhymes of different sorts; they are connected with the serious art of poetry which had its own 'toys and trifles'—such feats of skill in verse and rhyming as Chaucer shows in his *Complaint of Anelida*. Tricks of verse were apt to multiply as the poetic imagination failed—a substitute for poetry; but many of the strongest poets have used them occasionally. Among all the artistic games one of the most curious is where a Welsh poet (in Oxford in the fifteenth century) gives a display of Welsh poetical form with English words—to confute the ignorant Saxon who had said there was no art of poetry in Wales.

The stanza forms in the Harleian book are various, and interesting to compare with modern stanzas. There is an example of the verse which has travelled from William of Poitiers, about the year 1100, to Burns and his imitators. Modern poetry begins with William of Poitiers using the verse of Burns in a poem on *Nothing*—

> The song I make is of no thing,
> Of no one, nor myself, I sing,
> Of joyous youth, nor love-longing,
>   Nor place, nor time;
> I rode on horseback, slumbering:
>   There sprang this rhyme!

Two hundred years after, it is found in England—

> Her eye hath wounded me, y-wisse,
> Her bende browen that bringeth blisse;
> Her comely mouth that mightè kisse
>   In mirth he were;
> I woldè chaungè mine for his
>   That is her fere!

tive ballad was most in favour where people were fondest
The love-song or the nonsense verses could not be kept
something more was wanted, and this was given by the
as the story was always dramatic, more or less, with
ople speaking, the entertainment was all the better. If
e whole explanation, it still accounts for something in
nd it is certainly true of some places where the ballad
d longest. The *carole* has lasted to the present day in
lands, together with some very ancient types of tune;
e ballads are much longer than in other countries,
ancers are unwearied and wish to keep it up as long as
e ballads are spun out, enormously.

y of ballad poetry in Western Europe, if one dates it
inning of the French *carole* fashion—about 1100—is
history of pure lyric, and to the history of romance. It
both, and related to both. There are many mysterious
he strangest thing of all is that it often seems to repeat
ely modern times—in the second half of the Middle
as been generally held to be the process by which epic
There is reason for thinking that epic poetry began
yric, something like the ballad chorus. The oldest
eroic poem, *Widsith*, is near to lyric; *Deor's Lament*
refrain. The old Teutonic narrative poetry (as in
have grown out of a very old sort of ballad custom,
tive elements increased and gradually killed the lyric,
n of a story by the minstrel took the place of the
However that may be, it is certain that the ballads
in the Middle Ages are related in a strange way to
etry, not by derivation, but by sympathy. The ballad
e same manner as the epic poets and choose by pre-
e kind of plot. The plots of epics are generally the
s. This is one of the great differences between the
oic poetry and the later romances. It is a difference
romances and the ballads. Few of the romances are
ry of Tristram and the story of King Arthur are
romantic poets are beaten by the story of Tristram,
ly keep away from the tragedy of Arthur. The

The romance stanza is used also in its original lyrical way, with a refrain added—

> For her love I cark and care
> For her love I droop and dare
> For her love my bliss is bare
>   And all I waxè wan;
> For her love in sleep I slake,
> For her love all night I wake
> For her love mourning I make
>   More than any man.
> *Blow, northern wind!*
> *Send thou me my sweeting!*
> *Blow, northern wind!*
> *Blow! blow! blow!*

Technically, it is to be noted that some of those poems have the combination of a six-line with a four-line passage which is frequent in French lyrics of all ages, which is also found in the verse of *The Cherrie and the Slae* (another of Burns's favourite measures), and also in some of Gray's simpler odes. It is found in one of the religious poems, with the six lines first, and the four lines after, as in Burns. The common French pattern arranges them the other way round, and so does Gray, but the constituent parts are the same.

> Now shrinketh rose and lily flower
> That whilom bare that sweete savour,
>   In summer, that sweete tide;
> Ne is no queene so stark ne stour,
> Ne no lady so bright in bower
>   That death ne shall by glide;
> Whoso will flesh-lust forgon,
>   And heaven bliss abide,
> On Jesu be his thought anon,
>   That thirled was his side.

This poem is a good text to prove the long ancestry of modern verse, and the community of the nations, often very remote from definite intercourse between them. And there is one phrase in this stanza which goes back to the older world: 'bright in bower' is from the ancient heroic verse; it may be found in Icelandic, in the Elder Edda.

The fifteenth century, which is so dismal in the works of the more ambitious poets (Lydgate, and Occleve, e.g.), is rich in popular carols which by this time have drawn close to the modern meaning of the name. They are Christmas carols, and the name loses its old general application to any song that went with dancing in a round. In the carols, the art is generally much more simple than in the lyrics which have just been quoted; they belong more truly to the common people, and their authors are less careful. Yet the difference is one of degree. The only difference which is really certain is between one poem and another.

Speaking generally about the carols one may say truly they are unlike the work of the Chaucerian school; the lyrics of the Harleian book in the reign of Edward I are nearer the Chaucerian manner. It is hardly worth while to say more, for the present.

And it is not easy to choose among the carols. Some of them are well known today—

> When Christ was born of Mary free
> In Bethlehem that fair city
> Angels sang loud with mirth and glee
> *In excelsis gloria.*

Ballads in the ordinary sense of the term—ballads with a story in them, like *Sir Patrick Spens* or *The Mill-dams of Binnorie*—are not found in any quantity till late in the Middle Ages, and hardly at all before the fifteenth century. But there are some early things of the kind. A rhyme of *Judas* (thirteenth century) is reckoned among the ballads by the scholar (the late Professor Child) who gave most time to the subject, and whose great collection of the English and Scottish Popular Ballads has brought together everything ascertainable about them.

By some the ballads are held to be degenerate romances; and they appear at a time when the best of romance was over, and when even the worst was dying out. Also, it is quite certain that some ballads are derived from romances. There is a ballad of the young *Hynd Horn* which comes from the old narrative poem of *King Horn* or of

---

Horn Childe. There is a ballad
which has been described in
difficulties in the way of this th
ballads which have no roman
may not prove much, for mar
one is to make allowance for
ballads may have been lost
back to the thirteenth cent
forms. Again, there are balla
of as existing in the shape o
ballad is lyrical; all ballads
any rate would lose their m
into a story. What would t
it were told in any other
about Dunfermline, the
Norway, and the manners
ballads are degenerate ron
known to be descended f
may be derived from a
corruption of any old na
form which has a value
not explain the form of
are explained by calling

The proper form of
narrative substance add
at a wake in a churchy
la Rose, or at Christm
and the Green Knigh
with a refrain of *douc*
the same; there was
fresh lines of the so
refrain, most often i
after the second—

> Whe
> W
> A f
> A

The narr
of dancing.
up so long;
story; also
different pe
this is not t
the history,
has flourishe
the Faroe Is
and there th
because the
may be. So t

The histor
from the beg
parallel to the
is distinct fro
things in it. T
in comparativ
Ages—what h
poetry begins.
in concerted
Anglo-Saxon h
is lyric, with
Beowulf) may
where the narr
so that recitati
dancing chorus
of Christendom
the older epic po
poets think in tl
ference the sam
plots of tragedie
Anglo-Saxon he
also between the
tragical. The st
tragical; but the
and they genera

ballads often have happy endings, but not nearly so often as the romances; in the best of the ballads there is a sorrowful ending; in many there is a tragical mistake; in many (and in how few of the romances!) there is a repetition of the old heroic scene, the last resistance against the enemy as in Roncevaux or in the *Nibelunge Nôt. Chevy Chase* is the ballad counterpart of *Maldon*; *Parcy Reed* or *Johnny of Braidislee* answers in the ballad form to the fight at *Finnesburh*, a story of a treacherous onset and a good defence. Parcy Reed, beset and betrayed, is more like a northern hero than a knight of romance.

The mystery is that the same kind of choice should be found in all the countries where ballads were sung. The English and Scottish ballads, like the English romances, are related to similar things in other lands. To understand the history of the ballads it is necessary, as with the romances, to compare different versions of the same matter—French or German, Italian, Danish.

Many curious things have been brought out by study of this sort—resemblances of ballad plots all over Christendom. But there is a sort of resemblance which no amount of 'analogues' in different languages can explain, and that is the likeness in temper among the ballad poets of different languages, which not only makes them take up the same stories, but makes them deal with fresh realities in the same way. How is it that an English ballad poet sees the death of Parcy Reed in a certain manner, while a Danish poet far off will see the some poetical meaning in a Danish adventure, and will turn it into the common ballad form? In both cases it is the death of a hero that the poet renders in verse; deaths of heroes are a subject for poetry, it may be said, all over the world. But how is it that this particular form should be used in different countries for the same kind of subject, not conventionally, but with imaginative life, each poet independently seizing this as the proper subject and treating it with all the force of his mind?

The medieval ballad is a form used by poets with their eyes open upon life, and with a form of thought in their minds by which they comprehend a tragic situation. The medieval romance is a form used originally by poets with a certain vein of sentiment who found that narrative plots helped them to develop their emotional rhetoric; then it passed through various stages in different countries, sinking into chapbooks or rising to the *Orlando* or the *Faerie Queene*—but never coming back to the old tragic form of imagination, out of which the older epics had been derived, and which is constantly found in the ballads.

Probably the old ballad chorus in its proper dancing form was going out of use in England about 1400. Barbour, a contemporary of Chaucer, speaks of girls singing ballads 'at their play'; Thomas Deloney in the time of Elizabeth describes the singing of a ballad refrain; and the game lives happily still, in songs of *London Bridge* and others. But it became more and more common for ballads to be sung or recited to an audience sitting still; ballads were given out by minstrels, like the minstrel of *Chevy Chase*. Sometimes ballads are found swelling into something like a narrative poem; such is the famous ballad of *Adam Bell, Clim o' the Clough, and William of Cloudeslee*, which has a plot of the right sort, the defence of a house against enemies. *The Little Geste of Robin Hood* seems to be an attempt to make an epic poem by joining together a number of ballads. The ballad of *Robin Hood's Death* is worth reading as a contrast to this rather mechanical work. *Robin Hood's Death* is a ballad tragedy; again, the death of a hero beset by traitors. Red Roger stabbed Robin with a grounden glave ('grounden' comes from the oldest poetic vocabulary). Robin made 'a wound full wide' between Roger's head and his shoulders. Then he asks Little John for the sacrament, the housel of earth (he call it 'moud', i.e. 'mould') which could be given and taken by any Christian man, in extremity, without a priest—

> 'Now give me moud,' Robin said to Little John,
> 'Now give me moud with thy hand;
> I trust to God in heaven so high
> My housel will me bestand.'

And he refuses to let Little John burn the house of the treacherous Prioress where he had come by his death. This is heroic poetry in its simplest form, and quite true to its proper nature.

The beauty of the ballads is uncertain and often corrupted by forgetfulness and the ordinary accidents of popular tradition. It is not

always true that the right subject has the best form. But the grace
of the ballads is unmistakable; it is unlike anything in the contemporary romances, because it is lyrical poetry. It is often vague
and intangible. It is never the same as narrative romance.

> He's tane three locks o' her yellow hair,
>   *Binnorie, O Binnorie!*
> And wi' them strung his harp so fair
>   *By the bonny mill-dams o' Binnorie.*

It is the singing voice that makes the difference; and it is a difference
of thought as well as of style.

6
Comic Poetry

FRANCE SETS THE model for comic as well as romantic poetry, in the Middle Ages. In romance the English were not able for a long time—hardly before Chaucer and Gower—to imitate the French style properly; the French sentiment was beyond them, not appreciated; they took the stories, the action and adventures, and let the sentiment alone, or abridged it. The reasons for this are obvious. But there seems to be no reason, except accident, for the way in which the English writers in those times neglected the French comic literature of the twelfth century. Very little of it is represented in the English of the following centuries; yet what there is in English corresponding to the French *fabliaux* and to Reynard the Fox is thoroughly well done. The English wit was quite equal to the French in matters such as these; there were no difficulties of style or caste in the way, such as prevented the English minstrels from using much of the French romantic, sentimental rhetoric. There might have been a thirteenth-century English *Reynard*, as good as the High or Low German *Reynards*; that is proved by the one short example (295 lines) in which an episode of the great medieval comic epic is told by an English versifier—the story of *The Vox and the Wolf*. This is one of the best of all the practical jokes of Reynard—the well-known story of the Fox and the Wolf in the well. It is told again, in a different way, among the Fables of the Scottish poet Robert Henryson; it is also one of the stories of Uncle Remus.

A vox gan out of the wodè go,

and made his way to a hen-roost, where he got three hens out of five, and argued with Chauntecler the cock, explaining, though unsuccessfully, that a little blood-letting might be good for him; thence, being troubled with thirst, he went to the well. The well had two buckets on a rope over a pulley; the Fox 'ne understood nought of the gin' and got into one of the buckets and went down to the bottom of the well; where he repented of his gluttony. The comic epic is as moral as Piers Plowman; that is part of the game.

Then ('out of the depe wode') appeared the Wolf, Sigrim (Isengrim), also thirsty, and looking for a drink; he heard the lamentations of his gossip Reneuard, and sat down by the well and called to him. Then at last the Fox's wit returned and he saw how he might escape. There was nothing (he said) he would have prayed for more than that his friend should join him in the happy place: 'here is the bliss of Paradise'. 'What! art thou dead?' says the Wolf: 'this is news; it was only three days ago that thou and thy wife and children all came to dine with me.' 'Yes! I am dead,' says the Fox. 'I would not return to the world again, for all the world's wealth. Why should I walk in the world, in care and woe, in filth and sin? But this place is full of all happiness; here is mutton, both sheep and goat.' When the Wolf heard of this good meat his hunger overcame him and he asked to be let in. 'Not till thou art shriven,' says the Fox; and the Wolf bends his head, sighing hard and strong, and makes his confession, and gets forgiveness, and is happy.

> Nou ich am in clene live
> Ne recche ich of childe ne of wive.

'But tell me what to do.' 'Do!' quoth the Fox, 'leap into the bucket, and come down.' And the Wolf going down met the Fox half-way; Reynard, 'glad and blithe' that the Wolf was a true penitent and in clean living, promised to have his soul-knell rung and masses said for him.

The well, it should be said, belonged to a house of friars; Aylmer the 'master curtler' who looked after the kitchen-garden came to the well in the morning; and the Wolf was pulled out and beaten and hunted; he found no bliss and no indulgence of blows.

The French story has some points that are not in the English; in
the original, the two buckets on the pulley are explained to Isengrim
as being God's balance of good and evil, in which souls are weighed.
Also there is a more satisfactory account of the way Reynard came
to be entrapped. In the English story the failure of his wit is rather
disgraceful; in the French he takes to the bucket because he thinks
he sees his wife Hermeline in the bottom of the well; it is a clear
starlight night, and as he peers over the rim of the well he sees the
figure looking up at him, and when he calls there is a hollow echo
which he takes for a voice answering. But there is no such difference
of taste and imagination here between the French and the English
Reynard as there is between the French and the English chivalrous
romances.

The *Roman de Renart* is generally, and justly, taken as the ironical
counterpart of medieval epic and romance; an irreverent criticism of
dignitaries, spiritual and temporal, the great narrative comedy of the
Ages of Faith and of Chivalry. The comic short stories usually called
fabliaux are most of them much less intelligent; rhyming versions of
ribald jokes, very elementary. But there are great differences among
them, and some of them are worth remembering. It is a pity there is
no English version of the *jongleur*, the professional minstrel, who,
in the absence of the devils, is put in charge of the souls in Hell, but
is drawn by St. Peter to play them away at a game of dice—the result
being that he is turned out; since then the Master Devil has given
instructions: No Minstrels allowed within.

There are few English *fabliaux*; there is perhaps only one preserved as a separate piece by itself, the story of *Dame Sirith*. This is
far above the ordinary level of such things; it is a shameful practical
joke, but there is more in it than this; the character of Dame Sirith,
in her machinations to help the distressed lover of his neighbour's
wife, is such as belongs to comedy and to satire, not to the ordinary
vulgar 'merry tale'.

It is hard to find any other separate tale of this class in English;
but the stories of the Seven Wise Masters, the Seven Sages of Rome,
are many of them impossible to distinguish from the common type
of the French *fabliaux*, though they are often classed among the
romances. There are many historical problems connected with the

medieval short stories. Although they do not appear in writing to any large extent before the French rhyming versions, they are known to have been current long before the twelfth century and before the French language was used in literature. There are Latin versions of some of them composed in Germany before the *fabliaux* had come into existence; one of them in substance is the same as Hans Andersen's story of Big Claus and Little Claus, which also is found as one of the *fabliaux*. Evidently, there are a number of comic stories which have been going about for hundreds (or thousands) of years without any need of a written version. At any time, in any country, it may occur to some one to put one of those stories into literary language. Two of the German-Latin comic poems are in elaborate medieval verse, set to religious tunes, in the form of the *Sequentia* —a fact which is mentioned here only to show that there was nothing popular in these German experiments. They were not likely to found a school of comic story-telling; they were too difficult and exceptional; literary curiosities. The French *fabliaux*, in the ordinary short couplets and without any literary ornament, were absolutely popular; it needed no learning and not much wit to understand them. So that, as they spread and were circulated, they came often to be hardly distinguishable from the traditional stories which had been going about all the time in spoken, not written, forms. It was one of the great popular successes of medieval French literature; and it was due partly to the French stories themselves, and partly to the example which they set, that comic literature was cultivated in the later Middle Ages. The French stories were translated and adapted by Boccaccio and many others; and when the example had once been given, writers in different languages could find stories of their own without going to the *fabliaux*.

Does it matter much to any one where these stories came from, and how they passed from oral tradition into medieval (or modern) literary forms? The question is more reasonable than such questions usually are, because most of these stories are trivial, they are not all witty, and many of them are villainous. But the historical facts about them serve to bring out, at any rate, the extraordinary talent of the French for making literary profit out of every kind of material. Any one might have thought of writing out these stories which every one knew; but, with the exception of the few Latin experiments, this was done by nobody till the French took it up.

Further, those 'merry tales' come into the whole subject of the relations between folk-lore and literature, which is particularly important (for those who like that sort of inquiry) in the study of the Middle Ages. All the fiction of the Middle Ages, comic or romantic, is full of things which appear in popular tales like those collected by Grimm in Germany or by Campbell of Islay in the West Highlands. So much of medieval poetry is traditional or popular—the ballads especially—that folk-lore has to be studied more carefully than is needful when one is dealing with later times. With regard to short comic tales of the type of the *fabliaux*, part of the problem is easy enough, if one accepts the opinion that stories like *Big Claus and Little Claus*, which are found all over the world, and which can be proved to have been current orally for centuries, are things existing, and travelling, independently of written books, which may at any time be recorded in a written form. The written form may be literary, as when the story is written in Latin verse by an early German scholar, or in French medieval verse by a minstrel or a minstrel's hack, or in fine Danish prose by Hans Andersen. Or it may be written down by a scientific collector of folk-lore keeping closely to the actual phrasing of the unsophisticated story-teller; as when the plot is found among the Ananzi stories of the Negroes in the West Indies. The life of popular stories is mysterious; but it is well known in fact, and there is no difficulty in understanding how the popular story which is perennial in every climate may any day be used for the literary fashion of that day.

It is rather strange that while there is so much folk-lore in medieval literature there should be so few medieval stories which take up exactly the plots of any of the popular traditional tales. And it is a curious coincidence that two of the plots from folk-lore which are used in medieval literature, distinctly, by themselves, keeping to the folk-lore outlines, should also appear in literary forms equally distinct and no less true to their traditional shape among the Tales of Andersen. One is that which has just been mentioned, *Big Claus and Little Claus*, which comes into English rather late in the Middle Ages as the *Friars of Berwick*. The other is the *Travelling Com-*

panion, which in English rhyming romance is called *Sir Amadace*. There is something fortunate about those two stories which has gained for them more attention than the rest. They both come into the Elizabethan theatre, where again it is curiously rare to find a folk-lore plot. One is Davenport's *New Trick to Cheat the Devil*; the other, the *Travelling Companion*, is Peele's *Old Wives' Tale*.

With most of the short stories it is useless to seek for any definite source. To ask for the first author of *Big Claus and Little Claus* is no more reasonable than to ask who was the inventor of High Dutch and Low Dutch. But there is a large section of medieval story-telling which is in a different condition, and about which it is not wholly futile to ask questions of pedigree. *The Seven Sages of Rome* is the best example of this class; it has been remarked already that many things in the book are like the *fabliaux*; but unlike most of the *fabliaux* they have a literary origin which can be traced. The Book of the Seven Wise Masters of Rome (which exists in many different forms, with a variety of contents) is an Oriental collection of stories in a framework; that is to say, there is a plot which leads to the telling of stories, as in the *Arabian Nights*, the *Decameron*, the *Canterbury Tales*. The *Arabian Nights* were not known in the West till the beginning of the eighteenth century, but the Oriental plan of a group of stories was brought to Europe at least as early as the twelfth century. The plot of the *Seven Sages* is that the son of the Emperor of Rome is falsely accused by his stepmother, and defended by the Seven Masters, the Empress and the Masters telling stories against one another. As the object of the Masters is to prove that women are not to be trusted, it may be understood that their stories generally agree in their moral with the common disrespectful 'merry tales'. Among the lady's stories are some of a different complexion; one of these is best known in England through W. R. Spencer's ballad of the death of Gelert, the faithful hound who saved the child of his lord, and was hastily and unjustly killed in error. Another is the story of the Master Thief, which is found in the second book of Herodotus—the treasure of Rhampsinitus, king of Egypt.

One of those Oriental fables found among the old French short stories comes into English long afterwards in the form of Parnell's *Hermit*.

M E L—D

Although the *fabliaux* are not very largely represented in medieval English rhyme, there is a considerable amount of miscellaneous comic verse. One of the great differences between Middle English and Anglo-Saxon writings (judging from what is extant) is that in Middle English there is far more jesting and nonsense. The best of the comic pieces is one that might be reckoned along with the *fabliaux* except that there is no story in it; the description of the *Land of Cockayne*, sometimes called the land of Readymade, where the geese fly about roasted—

> Yet I do you mo to wit
> The geese y-roasted on the spit
> Fleeth to that abbey, Got it wot
> And gredeth: Geese all hot, all hot!

The land of Cockayne is a burlesque Paradise 'far in the sea by West of Spain'.

> There beth rivers great and fine
> Of oil, milk, honey and wine;
> Water serveth there to no thing,
> But to sight and to washing.

This piece, and *Reynard and Isengrim (The Fox and the Wolf)*, and others, show that fairly early, and before the French language had given way to English as the proper speech for good society, there was some talent in English authors for light verse, narrative or descriptive, for humorous stories, and for satire. The English short couplets of those days—of the time of Henry III and Edward I—are at no disadvantage as compared with the French. Anything can be expressed in that familiar verse which is possible in French—anything, except the finer shades of sentiment, for which as yet the English have no mind, and which must wait for the authors of the *Confessio Amantis* and the *Book of the Duchess Blanche*.

But there is one early poem—a hundred, it may be a hundred and fifty, years before Chaucer—in which not the sentiment but something much more characteristic of Chaucer is anticipated in a really wonderful way. *The Owl and the Nightingale* is an original poem, written in the language of Dorset at a time when nothing English was considered 'courteous'. Yet it is hard to see what is wanting to the poem to distinguish it from the literature of polite society in the Augustan ages. What is there provincial in it, except the language? And why should the language be called, except in a technical and literal sense, rustic, when it is used with a perfect command of idiom, with tact and discretion, with the good humour that comprehends many different things and motives at once, and the irony which may be a check on effusive romance, but never a hindrance to grace and beauty? Urbanity is the right word, the name one cannot help using, for the temper of this rustic and provincial poem. It is urbane, like Horace or Addison, without any town society to support the author in his criticism of life. The author is like one of the personages in his satire, the Wren, who was bred in the greenwood, but brought up among mankind—in the humanities:

> For theih heo were ybred a wolde
> Heo was ytowen among mankenne,
> And hire wisdom broughte thenne.

The Owl and the Nightingale is the most miraculous piece of writing, or, if that is too strong a term, the most contrary to all preconceived opinion, among the medieval English books. In the condition of the English language in the reign of Henry III, with so much against it, there was still no reason why there should not be plenty of English romances and a variety of English songs, though they might not be the same sort of romances and songs as were composed in countries like France or Germany, and though they might be wanting in the 'finer shades'. But all the chances, as far as we can judge, were against the production of humorous impartial essays in verse. Such things are not too common at any time. They were not common even in French polite literature in the thirteenth century. In the century after, Froissart in French, Gower and of course Chaucer in English have the same talent for light familiar rhyming essays that is shown by Prior and Swift. The early English poet had discovered for himself a form which generally requires ages of training and study before it can succeed.

His poem is entitled in one of the two MSS. *altercatio inter Philomenam et Bubonem*: 'A debate between the Nightingale and the Owl.' Debates, contentions, had been a favourite literary device for a long time in many languages. It was known in Anglo-Saxon poetry. It was common in France. There were contentions of Summer and Winter, of the Soul and the Body, the Church and the Synagogue, of Fast and Feasting; there were also (especially in the Provençal school) debates between actual men, one poet challenging another. The originality of *The Owl and the Nightingale* argument is that it is not, like so many of those poetical disputations, simply an arrangement of all the obvious commonplaces for and against one side and the other. It is a true comedy; not only is the writer impartial, but he keeps the debate alive; he shows how the contending speakers feel the strokes, and hide their pain, and do their best to face it out with the adversary. Also, the debate is not a mere got-up thing. It is Art against Philosophy; the Poet meeting the strong though not silent Thinker, who tells him of the Immensities and Infinities. The author agrees with Plato and Wordsworth that the nightingale is 'a creature of a fiery heart', and that the song is one of mirth and not lamentation. Yet it is not contrasted absolutely with the voice of the contemplative person. If it were, the debate would come to an end, or would turn into mere railing accusations—of which there is no want, it may be said, along with the more serious arguments. What makes the dispute worth following, what lifts it far above the ordinary medieval conventions, is that each party shares something of the other's mind. The Owl wishes to be thought musical; the Nightingale is anxious not to be taken for a mere worldling.

7
Allegory

ALLEGORY IS OFTEN taken to be the proper and characteristic mode of thought in the Middle Ages, and certainly there is no kind of invention which is commoner. The allegorical interpretation of Scripture was the regular, the universal method employed by preachers and commentators. Anglo-Saxon religious writings are full of it. At the Revival of Learning, five hundred years after Ælfric, the end of the Middle Ages is marked by a definite attack upon the allegorical method, an attack carried on by religious reformers and classical scholars, who held that allegory perverted and destroyed the genuine teaching of Scripture, and the proper understanding of Virgil and Ovid.

The book in which this medieval taste is most plainly exhibited is the *Gesta Romanorum*, a collection of stories, in Latin prose, drawn from many different sources, each story having the moral interpretation attached to it, for the use of preachers.

One of the most popular subjects for moral interpretation was natural history. There is a book called *Physiologus*—'the Natural Philosopher'—which went through all the languages in the same way as the story of Alexander or the book of the Seven Wise Masters. There are fragments of an Anglo-Saxon rendering, in verse—the *Whale*, and the *Panther*, favourite examples. The Whale is the Devil; the Whale lying in the sea with his back above water is often mistaken by sailors for an island; they land on his back to rest, and the Whale goes down with them to the depths. The common name for these natural histories (versions or adaptations of *Physiologus*) is 'Bestiary'; there is an English *Bestiary* of the beginning of the thirteenth century, most of it in the irregular alliterative verse which seems to have been common at that date; some of it is in fairly regular rhyme.

Allegorical interpretation of Scripture, or of stories, or of natural history is not the same thing as allegorical invention. This is sometimes forgotten, but it is clear enough that an allegory such as the *Pilgrim's Progress* has a quite different effect on the mind, and requires a different sort of imagination, from the allegorical work which starts from a given text and spins out some sort of moral from it. Any one with a little ingenuity can make an allegorical interpretation of any matter. It is a different thing to invent and carry on an allegorical story. One obvious difference is that in the first case—for example in the *Bestiary*—the two meanings, literal and allegorical, are separate from one another. Each chapter of the *Bestiary* is in two parts; first comes the *nature* of the beast—*natura leonis, etc.*—the natural history of the lion, the ant, the whale, the panther and so forth; then comes the *signification*. In the other kind of allegory, though there is a double meaning, there are not two separate meanings presented one after the other to the mind. The signification is given along with, or through, the scene and the figures. Christian in the *Pilgrim's Progress* is not something different from the Christian man whom he represents allegorically; Mr. Greatheart, without any interpretation at all, is recognized at once as a courageous guide and champion. So when the Middle Ages are blamed for their allegorical tastes it may be well to distinguish between the frequently mechanical allegory which forces a moral out of any object, and the imaginative allegory which puts fresh pictures before the mind. The one process starts from a definite story or fact, and then destroys the story to get at something inside; the other makes a story and asks you to accept it and keep it along with its allegorical meaning.

Thus allegorical invention, in poetry like Spenser's, or in imaginative prose like Bunyan's, may be something not very different from imaginative work with no conscious allegory in it at all. All poetry has something of a representative character in it, and often it matters little for the result whether the composer has any definite symbolic intention or not. *Beowulf* or *Samson Agonistes* might be said to 'stand for' heroism, just as truly as the Red Cross Knight in Spenser, or Mr. Valiant for Truth in the *Pilgrim's Progress*. So in studying medieval allegories either in poetry, painting or sculpture, it seems advisable to consider in each case how far the artist has strained his imagination to serve an allegorical meaning, or whether he has not succeeded in being imaginative with no proper allegorical meaning at all.

By far the best known and most influential of medieval allegories is the *Romance of the Rose*. Both in France and in England it kept its place as a poetical example and authority from the thirteenth century till well on in the sixteenth. It is the work of two authors; the later, Jean Clopinel or Jean de Meung, taking up the work of Guillaume de Lorris about 1270, forty years after the death of the first inventor. The part written by Jean Clopinel is a rambling allegorical satire, notorious for its slander against women. The earlier part, by Guillaume de Lorris, is what really made the fame and spread the influence of the *Roman de la Rose*, though the second part was not far below it in importance.

Guillaume de Lorris is one of those authors, not very remarkable for original genius, who put together all the favourite ideas and sentiments of their time in one book from which they come to be distributed widely among readers and imitators. His book is an allegory of all the spirit and doctrine of French romantic poetry for the past hundred years; and as the French poets had taken all they could from the lyric poets of Provence, the *Roman de la Rose* may be fairly regarded as an abstract of the Provençal lyrical ideas almost as much as of French sentiment. It was begun just at the time when the Provençal poetry was ended in the ruin of the South and of the Southern chivalry, after the Albigensian crusade.

No apology is needed for speaking of this poem in a discourse on English literature. Even if Chaucer had not translated it, the *Roman de la Rose* would still be a necessary book for any one who wishes to understand not only Chaucer but the poets of his time and all his successors down to Spenser. The influence of the *Roman de la Rose* is incalculable. It is acknowledged by the poet whose style is least like Chaucer's, except for its liveliness, among all the writers in the reign of Edward III—by the author of the alliterative poem on *Purity*, who is also generally held to be the author of the *Pearl* and of *Sir Gawayne*, and who speaks with respect of 'Clopyngel's clene rose'.

It is thoroughly French in all its qualities—French of the thirteenth century, using ingeniously the ideas and the form best suited to the readers whom it sought to win.

One of the titles of the *Roman de la Rose* is the *Art of Love*. The name is taken from a poem of Ovid's which was a favourite with more than one French poet before Guillaume de Lorris. It appealed to them partly on account of its subject, and partly because it was a didactic poem. It suited the common medieval taste for exposition of doctrine, and the *Roman de la Rose* which follows it and copies its title is a didactic allegory. In every possible way, in its plan, its doctrine, its sentiment, its decoration and machinery, the *Roman de la Rose* collects all the things that had been approved by literary tradition and conveys them, with their freshness renewed, to its successors. It concludes one period; it is a summary of the old French romantic and sentimental poetry, a narrative allegory setting forth the ideas that might be extracted from Provençal lyric. Then it became a storehouse from which those ideas were carried down to later poets, among others to Chaucer and the Chaucerian school. Better than anything else, the descriptive work in the *Roman de la Rose* brings out its peculiar success as an intermediary between earlier and later poets. The old French romantic authors had been fond of descriptions, particularly descriptions of pictorial subjects used as decoration, in painting or tapestry, for a magnificent room. The *Roman de la Rose*, near the beginning, describes the allegorical figures on the outside wall of the garden, and this long and elaborate passage, of the same kind as many earlier descriptions, became in turn, like everything else in the book, an example for imitation. How closely it is related to such arts as it describes was proved in Ruskin's *Fors Clavigera*, where along with his notes on the *Roman de la Rose* are illustrations from Giotto's allegorical figures in the chapel of the Arena at Padua.

The 'formal garden' of the Rose is equally true, inside the wall—

> The gardin was by mesuring
> Right even and squar in compassing.

The trees were set even, five fathom or six from one another.

> In places saw I wèlles there
> In whiche ther no froggès were
> And fair in shadwe was every welle;
> But I ne can the nombre telle
> Of stremès smale that by device
> Mirth had done comè through coundys,
> Of which the water in renning
> Can make a noyse ful lyking.

The dreamer finds Sir Mirth and a company of fair folk and fresh, dancing a *carole*.

> This folk of which I telle you so
> Upon a carole wenten tho;
> A lady caroled hem, that highte
> Gladnesse the blisful the lighte;
> Wel coude she singe and lustily,
> Non half so wel and semely,
> And make in song swich refreininge
> It sat her wonder wel to singe.

The dream, the May morning, the garden, the fair company, the carole all were repeated for three hundred years by poets of every degree, who drew from the *Romaunt of the Rose* unsparingly, as from a perennial fountain. The writers whom one would expect to be impatient with all things conventional, Chaucer and Sir David Lyndsay, give no sign that the May of the old French poet has lost its charm for them; though each on one occasion, Chaucer in the *Hous of Fame* and Lyndsay in the *Dreme*, with a definite purpose changes the time to winter. With both, the May comes back again, in the *Legend of Good Women* and in the *Monarchy*.

Even Petrarch, the first of the moderns to think contemptuously of the Middle Ages, uses the form of the Dream in his *Trionfi*—he lies down and sleeps on the grass at Vaucluse, and the vision follows, of the Triumph of Love.

The *Pearl*, one of the most beautiful of the English medieval poems, is an allegory which begins in this same way; the *Vision of Piers Plowman* is another. Neither of these has otherwise much likeness to the *Rose*; it was by Chaucer and his school that the authority of the *Rose* was established. The *Pearl* and *Piers Plowman* are original works, each differing very considerably from the French style which was adopted by Chaucer and Gower.

The *Pearl* is written in a lyrical stanza, or rather in groups of stanzas linked to one another by their refrains; the measure is unlike French verse. The poem itself, which in many details resembles many other things, is altogether quite distinct from anything else, and indescribable except to those who have read it. Its resemblance to the *Paradiso* of Dante is that which is less misleading than any other comparison. In the English poem, the dreamer is instructed as to the things of heaven by his daughter Marjory, the Pearl that he had lost, who appears to him walking by the river of Paradise and shows him the New Jerusalem; like Dante's Beatrice at the end she is caught away from his side to her place in glory.

But it is not so much in these circumstances that the likeness is to be found—it is in the fervour, the belief, which carries everything with it in the argument, and turns theology into imagination. As with Dante, allegory is a right name, but also an insufficient name for the mode of thought in this poem.

In the *Pearl* there is one quite distinct and abstract theory which the poem is intended to prove; a point of theology (possibly heretical): that all the souls of the blessed are equal in happiness; each one is queen or king. In *Sir Gawayne*, which is probably by the same author, there is the same kind of definite thought, never lost or confused in the details. *Piers Plowman,* on the other hand, though there are a number of definite things which the author wishes to enforce, is wholly different in method. The method often seems as if it were nothing at all but random association of ideas. The whole world is in the author's mind, experience, history, doctrine, the estates and fortunes of mankind, 'the mirror of middle-earth'; all the various elements are turned and tossed about, scenes from Bartholomew Fair mixed up with preaching or philosophy. There is the same variety, it may be said, in the *Pilgrim's Progress*. But there is not the same confusion. With Bunyan, whatever the conversation may be, there is always the map of the road quite clear.

You know where you are; and if ever the talk is abstract it is the talk of people who eat and drink and wear clothes—real men, as one is accustomed to call them. In *Piers Plowman* there is as much knowledge of life as in Bunyan; but the visible world is seen only from time to time. It is not merely that some part of the book is comic description and some of it serious discourse, but the form of thought shifts in a baffling way from the pictorial to the abstract. It is tedious to be told of a brook named 'Be buxom of speech', and a croft called 'Covet not men's cattle nor their wives', when nothing is made of the brook or the croft by way of scenery; the pictorial words add nothing to the moral meaning; if the Ten Commandments are to be turned into allegory, something more is wanted than the mere tacking on to them of a figurative name. The author of *Piers Plowman* is too careless, and uses too often a mechanical form of allegory which is little better than verbiage.

But there is more than enough to make up for that, both in the comic scenes like the Confession of the Seven Deadly Sins, and in the sustained passages of reasoning, like the argument about the righteous heathen and the hopes allowable to Saracens and Jews. The Seven Sins are not abstractions nor grotesque allegories; they are vulgar comic personages such as might have appeared in a comedy or a novel of low life, in London taverns or country inns, figures of tradesmen and commercial travellers, speaking the vulgar tongue, natural, stupid, ordinary people.

Also there is beauty; the poem is not to be dismissed as a long religious argument with comic interludes, though such a description would be true enough, as far as it goes. The author is no great artist, for he lets his meaning overpower him and hurry him, and interrupt his pictures and his story. But he is a poet, for all that, and he proves his gift from the outset of his work 'in a May morning, on Malvern hilles'; and with all his digressions and seemingly random thought the argument is held together and moves harmoniously in its large spaces. The secret of its construction is revealed in the long triumphant passage which renders afresh the story of the Harrowing of Hell, and in the transition to what follows, down to the end of the poem. The author has worked up to a climax in what may be called his drama of the Harrowing of Hell. This is given fully, and with a sense of its greatness, from the beginning when the voice and the light together break in upon the darkness of Hell and on the 'Dukes of that dim place'—*Attollite portas*: 'be ye lift up, ye everlasting doors'. After the triumph, the dreamer awakes and hears the bells on Easter morning—

> That men rongen to the resurrexioun, and right with that I waked
> And called Kitte my wyf and Kalote my doughter:
> Ariseth and reverenceth Goddes resurrexioun,
> And crepeth to the crosse on knees, and kisseth it for a juwel,
> For Goddes blessid body it bar for owre bote,
> And it afereth the fende, for suche is the myghte
> May no grysly gost glyde there it shadoweth!

This is the end of one vision, but it is not the end of the poem. There is another dream.

> I fel eftsones aslepe and sodeynly me mette
> That Pieres the plowman was paynted al blody
> And come on with a crosse before the comune people
> And righte lyke in alle lymes to oure lorde Jhesu
> And thanne called I Conscience to kenne me the sothe:
> 'Is this Jhesus the juster' quoth I 'that Jewes did to death
> Or is it Pieres the plowman? Who paynted him so rede?'
> Quoth Conscience and kneled tho: 'This aren Pieres armes,
> His coloures and his cote-armure, ac he that cometh so blody
> Is Cryst with his crosse, conqueroure of crystene'.

The end is far off; Antichrist is to come; Old Age and Death have their triumph likewise. The poem does not close with a solution of all problems, but with a new beginning; Conscience setting out on a pilgrimage. The poet has not gone wrong in his argument; the world is as bad as ever it was, and it is thus that he ends, after scenes of ruin that make one think of the Twilight of the Gods, and of the courage which the Northern heroes opposed to it.

It is not by accident that the story is shaped in this way. The construction is what the writer wished it to be, and his meaning is expressed with no failure in coherence. His mind is never satisfied;

least of all with such conclusions as would make him forget the distresses of human life. He is like Blake saying—

> I will not cease from mental fight
> Nor shall my sword sleep in my hand.

The book of *Piers Plowman* is found in many manuscripts which were classified by Mr. Skeat in his edition of the poem as representing three versions, made at different times by the author who twice revised his book, so that there is an earlier and a later revised and expanded version besides the first. This theory of the authorship is not accepted by every one, and attempts have been made to distinguish different hands, and more particularly to separate the authorship of the first from the second version. Those who wish to multiply the authors have to consider, among other things, the tone of thought in the poem; it is hard to believe that there were two authors in the same reign who had the same strong and weak points, the same inconsistencies, wavering between lively imagination and formal allegory, the same indignation and the same tolerance. *Piers Plowman* is one of the most impartial of all reformers. He makes heavy charges against many ranks and orders of men, but he always remembers the good that is to be said for them. His remedy for the evils of the world would be to bring the different estates—knights, clergy, labourers and all—to understand their proper duty. His political ideal is the commonwealth as it exists, only with each part working as it was meant to do: the king making the peace, with the knights to help him, the clergy studying and praying, the commons working honestly, and the higher estates also giving work and getting wages. In this respect there is no inconsistency between the earlier and the later text. In the second version he brings in Envy as the philosophical socialist who proves out of Plato and Seneca that all things should be in common. This helps to confirm what is taught in the first version about the functions of the different ranks. If the later versions are due to later hands, they, at any rate, continue and amplify what is taught in the first version, with no inconsistency.

8

Sermons and Histories, in Verse and Prose

It is one of the common difficulties in studying ancient literature that the things preserved are not always what we would have chosen. In modern literature, criticism and the opinion of the reading public have generally sorted out the books that are best worth considering; few authors are wrongfully neglected, and the well-known authors generally deserve their reputation. But in literature such as that of the thirteenth century, or the fourteenth before the time of Chaucer, not much has been done by the opinion of the time to sift out the good from the bad, and many things appear in the history of literature which are valuable only as curiosities, and some which have no title to be called books at all. The *Ayenbite of Inwit* is well known by name, and passes for a book; it is really a collection of words in the Kentish dialect, useful for philologists, especially for those who, like the author of the book, only care for one word at a time. The *Ayenbite of Inwit* was translated from the French by Dan Michel of Northgate, one of the monks of St. Augustine's at Canterbury, in 1340; it is extant in his own handwriting; there is no evidence that it was ever read by any one else. The method of the author is to take each French word and give the English for it; if he cannot read the French word, or mistakes it, he puts down the English for what he thinks it means, keeping his eye firmly fixed on the object, and refusing to be distracted by the other words in the sentence. This remarkable thing has been recorded in histories as a specimen of English prose.

The *Ormulum* is another famous work which is preserved only in the author's original handwriting. It is a different thing from the *Ayenbite*; it is scholarly in its own way, and as far as it goes it accomplishes all that the author set out to do. As it is one of the earliest books of the thirteenth century, it is immensely valuable as a document; not only does it exhibit the East Midland language of its time, in precise phonetic spelling (the three G's of the *Ormulum* are now famous in philology), but it contains a large amount of the best ordinary medieval religious teaching; and as for literature, its author was the first in English to use an exact metre with unvaried number of syllables; it has been described already. But all those merits do not make the *Ormulum* much more than a curiosity in the history of poetry—a very distinct and valuable sign of certain common tastes, certain possibilities of education, but it itself tasteless.

One of the generalities proved by the *Ormulum* is the use of new metres for didactic work. The Anglo-Saxon verse had been taken not infrequently for didactic purposes—at one time for the paraphrase of *Genesis*, at another for the moral emblems of the *Whale* and the *Panther*. But the Anglo-Saxon verse was not very well fitted for school books; it was too heavy in diction. And there was no need for it, with Anglo-Saxon prose established as it was. After the Norman Conquest, however, there was a change. Owing to the example of the French, verse was much more commonly used for ordinary educational purposes. There is a great deal of this extant, and the difficulty arises how to value it properly, and distinguish what is a document in the history of general culture, or morality, or religion, from what is a poem as well.

One of the earliest Middle English pieces is a Moral Poem which is found in several manuscripts and evidently was well known and popular. It is in the same metre as the *Ormulum*, but written with more freedom, and in rhyme. This certainly is valuable as a document. The contents are the ordinary religion and morality, the vanity of human wishes, the wretchedness of the present world, the fearfulness of Hell, the duty of every man to give up all his relations in order to save his soul. This commonplace matter is, however, expressed with great energy in good language and spirited verse; the irregularity of the verse is not helplessness, it is the English

freedom which keeps the rhythm, without always regularly obser-
ving the exact number of syllables.

> Ich am eldrè than ich was, a winter and eke on lorè,
> Ich weldè morè than ich dyde, my wit oughtè be morè.

i.e.—

> I am older than I was, in winters and also in learning;
> I wield more than I did [I am stronger than I once was], my wit
> ought to be more.

The first line, it will be noticed, begins on the strong syllable; the
weak syllable is dropped, as it is by Chaucer and Milton when they
think fit. With this freedom, the common metre is established as a
good kind of verse for a variety of subjects; and the *Moral Ode*, as it
is generally called, is therefore to be respected in the history of poetry.
One vivid thing in it seems to tell where the author came from. In
the description of the fire of Hell he says—

> Ne mai hit quenchè salt water, ne Avene stream ne Sture.

He is thinking of the rivers of Christchurch, and the sea beyond, as
Dante in Hell remembers the clear mountain waters running down
to the Arno.

Layamon's *Brut* shows how difficult it might be for an Englishman
in the reign of King John to find the right sort of verse. The matter
of the *Brut* is Geoffrey of Monmouth's history, originally in Latin
prose. This had been translated into French, and of course into
rhyme, because nothing but rhyme in French was thought a
respectable form. Layamon has the French rhyming version before
him, and naturally does not think of turning it into prose. That
would be mean, in comparison; once the historical matter has been
put into poetical form, it must not be allowed to fall back into any
form less honourable than the French. Layamon, however, has no
proper verse at command. He knows the old English alliterative
verse, but only in the corrupt variety which is found in some of the
later Anglo-Saxon pieces, with an increasing taste for rhyme;
Layamon, of course, had also in his head the rhymes of the French
couplets which he was translating; and the result is a most

disagreeable and discordant measure. The matter of Layamon in many places compensates for this; much of it, indeed, is heavy and prosaic, but some of it is otherwise, and the credit of the memorable passages is at least as often due to Layamon as to the original British history. He found the right story of the passing of Arthur, and that makes up for much of his uncomfortable verse and ranks him higher than the mere educational paraphrasers.

The *Bestiary* and the *Proverbs of Alfred* are two other works which resemble the *Brut* more or less in versification, and are interesting historically. It ought to be said, on behalf of the poorer things in this early time, that without exception they prove a very rich colloquial idiom and vocabulary, which might have been used to good effect, if any one had thought of writing novels, and which is in fact well used in many prose sermons, and, very notably, in the long prose book of the *Ancren Riwle*.

Looking at the *Ancren Riwle* and some other early prose, one is led to think that the French influence, so strong in every way, so distinctly making for advance in civilization, was hurtful to the English, and a bad example, in the literature of teaching, because the French had nothing equal to the English prose. French prose hardly begins till the thirteenth century; the history of Villehardouin is contemporary with the *Ancren Riwle*. But the English prose authors of that time were not beginners; they had the Anglo-Saxon prose to guide them, and they regularly follow the tradition of Ælfric. There is no break in the succession of prose as there is between Anglo-Saxon and Plantagenet verse; Anglo-Saxon prose did not lose its form as the verse did, and Ælfric, who was copied by English preachers in the twelfth century, might have taught something of prose style to the French, which they were only beginning to discover in the century after. And there might have been a thirteenth-century school of English prose, worthy of comparison with the Icelandic school of the same time, if the English had not been so distracted and overborne by the French example of didactic rhyme. French rhyme was far beyond any other model for romance; when it is used for historical or scientific exposition it is a poor and childish mode, incomparably weaker than the prose of Ælfric. But the example and the authority of the French didactic rhyme proved

too strong, and English prose was neglected; so much so that
the *Ancren Riwle*, a prose book written at the beginning of the
thirteenth century, is hardly matched even in the time of Chaucer
and Wycliffe; hardly before the date of Malory or Lord Berners.

The *Ancren Riwle* (the *Rule of Anchoresses*) is a book of doctrine
and advice, like many others in its substance. What distinguishes it
is the freshness and variety of its style. It is not, like so many
excellent prose works, a translation. The writer doubtless took his
arguments where he found them, in older books, but he thinks them
over in his own way, and arranges them; and he always has in mind
the one small household of religious ladies for whom he is writing,
their actual circumstances and the humours of the parish. His
literary and professional formulas do not get in his way; he sees the
small restricted life as it might have appeared to a modern essayist,
and writes of it in true-bred language, the style in which all honest
historians agree. The passages which are best worth quoting are
those which are oftenest quoted, about the troubles of the nun who
keeps a cow; the cow strays, and is pounded; the religious lady loses
her temper, her language is furious; then she has to beseech and
implore the heyward (parish beadle) and pay the damages after all.
Wherefore it is best for nuns to keep a cat only. But no one quotation can do justice to the book, because the subjects are varied, and
the style also. Much of it is conventional morality, some of it is
elementary religious instruction. There are also many passages
where the author uses his imagination, and in his figurative description of the Seven Deadly Sins he makes one think of the 'characters'
which were so much in fashion in the seventeenth century; there is
the same love of conceits, though not carried quite so far as in the
later days. The picture of the Miser as the Devil's own lubberly boy,
raking in the ashes till he is half blind, drawing 'figures of augrim'
in the ashes, would need very little change to turn it into the manner
of Samuel Butler, author of *Hudibras*, in his prose *Characters*; so
likewise the comparison of the envious and the wrathful man to the
Devil's jugglers, one making grotesque faces, the other playing with
knives. Elsewhere the writer uses another sort of imagination and a
different style; his description of Christ, in a figure drawn from
chivalry, is a fine example of eloquent preaching; how fine it is,

may be proved by the imitation of it called the *Wooing of Our Lord*, where the eloquence is pushed to an extreme. The author of the *Ancren Riwle* felt both the attraction and the danger of pathos; and he escaped the error of style into which his imitator fell; he kept to the limits of good prose. At the same time, there is something to be said in defence of the too poetic prose which is exemplified in the *Wooing of Our Lord*, and in other writings of that date. Some of it is derived from the older alliterative forms, used in the *Saints' Lives* of Ælfric; and this, with all its faults and excesses, at any rate kept an idea of rhythm which was generally wanting in the alliterative verse of the thirteenth century. It may be a wrong sort of eloquence, but it could not be managed without a sense of rhythm or beauty of words; it is not meagre or stinted, and it is in some ways a relief from the prosaic verse in which English authors copied the regular French couplets, and the plain French diction.

One of the best pieces of prose about this time is a translation from the Latin. *Soul's Ward* is a homily, a religious allegory of the defence of Man's Soul. The original Latin prose belongs to the mystical school of St. Victor in Paris. The narrative part of the English version is as good as can be; the mystical part, in the description of Heaven and the Beatific Vision, is memorable even when compared with the greatest masters, and keeps its own light and virtue even when set alongside of Plotinus or Dante. Here, as in the *Ancren Riwle*, the figures of eloquence, rhythm and alliteration are used temperately, and the phrasing is wise and imaginative; not mere ornament. By one sentence it may be recognized and remembered; where it is told how the souls of the faithful see 'all the redes and the runes of God, and his dooms that dern be, and deeper than any sea-dingle'.

The greatest loss in the transition from Anglo-Saxon to Norman and Angevin times was the discontinuance of prose history, and the failure of the Chronicle after the accession of Henry II. It made a good end. The Peterborough monk who did the reign of Stephen was much worse off for language than his predecessors either in the time of Edward the Elder or Edward the Confessor. His language is what he chooses to make it, without standard or control. But his narrative is not inferior in style to the best of the old work, though it is weaker in spelling. It is less restrained and more emotional than the Anglo-Saxon history; in telling of the lawlessness under King Stephen the writer cannot help falling into the tone of the preachers. In the earlier Chronicle one is never led to think about the sentiments of the writer; the story holds the attention. But here the personal note comes in; the author asks for sympathy. One thinks of the cold, gloomy church, the small depressed congregation, the lamentable tones of the sermon in the days when 'men said openly that Christ slept and his saints'. With the coming of Henry of Anjou a new order began, but the Chronicle did not go on; the monks of Peterborough had done their best, but there was no real chance for English prose history when it had come to depend on one single religious house for its continuance. The business was carried on in Latin prose and in French rhyme; through the example of the French, it became the fashion to use English verse for historical narrative, and it was long before history came back to prose.

Of all the rhyming historians Robert of Gloucester in the reign of Edward I is the most considerable by reason of style. Robert Manning of Brunne was more of a literary critic; the passage in which he deals severely with the contemporary rhyming dunces is singularly interesting in a time when literary criticism is rare. But Robert of Brunne is not so successful as Robert of Gloucester, who says less about the principles of rhyme, but discovers and uses the right kind. This was not the short couplet. The short couplet, the French measure, was indeed capable of almost anything in English, and it was brilliantly used for history by Barbour, and not meanly in the following century by Andrew Wyntoun. But it was in danger of monotony and flatness; for a popular audience a longer verse was better, with more swing in it. Robert of Gloucester took the 'common measure', with the ordinary accepted licences, as it is used by the ballad poets, and by some of the romances—for example, in the most admirable *Tale of Gamelyn*. He turns the history of Britain to the tune of popular minstrelsy, and if it is not very high poetry, at any rate it moves.

The same kind of thing was done about the same time with the *Lives of the Saints*—possibly some of them by Robert of Gloucester himself. These are found in many manuscripts, with many varia-

tions; but they are one book, the Legend, keeping the order of
Saints' Days in the Christian Year. This has been edited, under the
title of the *South English Legendary*, and there are few books in
which it is easier to make acquaintance with the heart and mind of
the people; it contains all sorts of matter: church history as in the
lives of St. Dunstan, St. Thomas of Canterbury and St. Francis 'the
Friar Minor'; and legend, in the common sense of the word, as in
the life of St. Eustace, or of St. Julian 'the good harbinger'. There
is the adventure of Owen the knight in St. Patrick's Purgatory;
there is also the voyage of St. Brandan. In one place there is a short
rhyming treatise on natural science, thoroughly good and sound,
and in some ways very modern. The right tone of the popular
science lecture has been discovered; and the most effective illustrations. The earth is a globe; night is the shadow of the earth; let us
take an apple and a candle, and everything is plain. Astronomical
distances are given in the usual good-natured manner of the lecturer
who wishes to stir but not to shock the recipient minds. The
cosmography, of course, is roughly that of Dante and Chaucer;
seven spheres beneath the eighth, which is the sphere of the fixed
stars and the highest visible heaven. The distance to that sphere
from the earth is so great that a man walking forty miles a day
could not reach it in eight thousand years. If Adam had started at
once at that rate, and kept it up, he would not be there yet—

Much is between heaven and earth; for the man that mightè go
Every day forty mile, and yet some deal mo,
He ne shoulde nought to the highest heaven, that ye alday y-seeth
Comen in eighte thousand year, there as the sterren beeth:
And though Adam our firstè father had begun anon
Tho that he was first y-made, and toward the heaven y-gon,
And had each day forty mile even upright y-go
He ne had nought yet to heaven y-come, by a thousand mile and mo!

Encyclopedias and universal histories are frequent in rhyme. The
Northern dialect comes into literary use early in the fourteenth
century in a long book, the *Cursor Mundi* or *Cursor o Werld*, which
is one of the best of its kind, getting fairly over the hazards of the
short couplet. In the Northern dialect this type of book comes to an

end two hundred years later; the *Monarchy* of Sir David Lyndsay is the last of its race, a dialogue between Experience and a Courtier, containing a universal history in the same octosyllabic verse as the *Cursor Mundi*. The Middle Ages may be dated as far down as this; it is a curiously old-fashioned and hackneyed form to be used by an author so original as Lyndsay, but he found it convenient for his anti-clerical satire. And it may be observed that generally the didactic literature of the Middle Ages varies enormously not only as between one author and another, but in different parts of the same work; nothing (except, perhaps, the *Tale of Melibeus*) is absolutely conventional repetition; passages of real life may occur at any moment.

The *Cursor Mundi* is closely related to the Northern groups of *Miracle Plays*. The dramatic scheme of the *Miracle Plays* was like that of the comprehensive narrative poem, intended to give the history of the world 'from Genesis to the day of Judgement'. It is impossible in this book to describe the early drama, its rise and progress; but it may be observed that its form is generally near to the narrative, and sometimes to the lyrical verse of the time.

The *Cursor Mundi* is one of a large number of works in the Northern dialect, which in that century was freely used for prose and verse—particularly by Richard Rolle of Hampole and his followers, a school whose mysticism is in contrast to the more scholastic method of Wycliffe. The most interesting work in the Northern language is Barbour's *Bruce*. Barbour, the Scottish contemporary of Chaucer, is not content with mere rhyming chronicles; he has a theory of poetry, he has both learning and ambition, which fortunately do not interfere much with the spirit of his story.

9
Chaucer

CHAUCER HAS SOMETIMES been represented as a French poet writing in English—not only a 'great translator' as his friend Eustache Deschamps called him, but so thoroughly in sympathy with the ideas and the style of French poetry that he is French in spirit even when he is original. This opinion about Chaucer is not the whole truth, but there is a great deal in it. Chaucer got his early literary training from French authors; particularly from the *Romance of the Rose*, which he translated, and from the poets of his own time or a little earlier: Machaut, Deschamps, Froissart, Granson. From these authors he learned the refinements of courtly poetry, the sentiment and the elegant phrasing of the French school, along with a number of conventional devices which were easier to imitate, such as the allegorical dream in the fashion of the *Roman de la Rose*. With Chaucer's poetry, we might say, English was brought up to the level of French. For two or three centuries English writers had been trying to be as correct as the French, but had seldom or never quite attained the French standard. Now the French were equalled in their own style by an English poet. English poetry at last comes out in the same kind of perfection as was shown in French and Provençal as early as the twelfth century, in German a little later with narrative poets such as Wolfram von Eschenbach, the author of *Parzival*, and lyric poets such as Walther von der Vogelweide. Italian was later still, but by the end of the thirteenth century, in the poets who preceded Dante, the Italian language proved itself at least the equal of the French and Provençal, which had ripened earlier. English was the last of the languages in which the poetical idea of the Middle Ages was realized—the ideal of courtesy and grace.

One can see that this progress in English was determined by some general conditions—the 'spirit of the age'. The native language had all along been growing in importance, and by the time of Chaucer French was no longer what it had been in the twelfth or thirteenth centuries, the only language fit for a gentleman. At the same time French literature retained its influence and its authority in England; and the result was the complete adaptation of the English language to the French manner of thought and expression. The English poetry of Gower is enough to prove that what Chaucer did was not all due to Chaucer's original genius, but was partly the product of the age and the general circumstances and tendencies of literature and education. Gower, a man of literary talent, and Chaucer, a man of genius, are found at the same time, working in the same way, with objects in common. Chaucer shoots far ahead and enters on fields where Gower is unable to follow him; but in a considerable part of Chaucer's work he is along with Gower, equally dependent on French authority and equally satisfied with the French perfection. If there had been no Chaucer, Gower would have had a respectable place in history as the one 'correct' English poet of the Middle Ages, as the English culmination of that courtly medieval poetry which had its rise in France and Provence two or three hundred years before. The prize for style would have been awarded to Gower; as it is, he deserves rather more consideration than he has generally received in modern times. It is easy to pass him over and to say that his correctness is flat, his poetical art monotonous. But at the very lowest valuation he did what no one else except Chaucer was able to do; he wrote a large amount of verse in perfect accordance with his own critical principles, in such a way as to stand minute examination; and in this he thoroughly expressed the good manners of his time. He proved that English might compete with the languages which had most distinguished themselves in poetry. Chaucer did as much; and in his earlier work he did no more than Gower.

The two poets together, different as they are in genius, work in common under the same conditions of education to gain for England the rank that had been gained earlier by the other countries—France and Provence, Germany and Italy. Without them, English poetry would have possessed a number of interesting, a number of beautiful medieval works, but nothing quite in the pure strain of the finest medieval art. English poetry would still have reflected in its mirror an immense variety of life, a host of dreams; but it would have wanted the vision of that peculiar courteous grace in which the French excelled. Chaucer and Gower made up what was lacking in English medieval poetry; the Middle Ages did not go by without a proper rendering of their finer spirit in English verse.

But a great many ages had passed before Chaucer and Gower appeared, and considered as spokesmen for medieval ideas they are rather belated. England never quite made up what was lost in the time of depression, in the century or two after the Norman Conquest. Chaucer and Gower do something like what was done by the authors of French romance in the twelfth century, such as Chrestien de Troyes, the author of *Enid*, or Benoît de Sainte More, the author of the *Romance of Troy*. But their writings do not alter the fact that England had missed the first freshness of chivalrous romance. There were two hundred years between the old French romantic school and Chaucer. Even the *Roman de la Rose* is a hundred years old when Chaucer translates it. The more recent French poets whom Chaucer translates or imitates are not of the best medieval period. Gower, who is more medieval than Chaucer, is a little behind his time. He is mainly a narrative poet, and narrative poetry had been exhausted in France; romances of adventure had been replaced by allegories (in which the narrative was little worth in comparison with the decoration), or, more happily, by familiar personal poems like those in which Froissart describes various passages in his own life. Froissart, it is true, the contemporary of Chaucer, wrote a long romance in verse in the old fashion; but this is the exception that proves the rule: Froissart's *Meliador* shows plainly enough that the old type of romance was done. It is to the credit of Gower that although he wrote in French a very long dull moralizing poem, he still in English kept in the main to narrative. It may have been old-fashioned, but it was a success.

Gower should always be remembered along with Chaucer; he is what Chaucer might have been without genius and without his Italian reading, but with his critical tact, and much of his skill in verse and diction. The *Confessio Amantis* is monotonous, but it is not dull. Much of it at a time is wearisome, but as it is composed of a number of separate stories, it can be read in bits, and ought to be so read. Taken one at a time the clear bright little passages come out with a meaning and a charm that may be lost when the book is read too perseveringly.

The *Confessio Amantis* is one of the medieval works in which a number of different conventions are used together. In its design it resembles the *Romance of the Rose*; and like the *Romance of the Rose* it belongs to the pattern of Boethius; it is in the form of a conversation between the poet and a divine interpreter. As a collection of stories, all held together in one frame, it follows the example set by *The Book of the Seven Wise Masters*. Like the *Romance of the Rose* again it is an encyclopedia of the art of love. Very fortunately, in some of the incidental passages it gets away from conventions and authorities, and enlarges in a modern good-tempered fashion on the vanities of the current time. There is more wickedness in Gower than is commonly suspected. Chaucer is not the only ironical critic of his age; and in his satire Gower appears to be, no less than Chaucer, independent of French examples, using his wit about the things and the humours which he could observe in the real life of his own experience.

Chaucer's life as a poet has by some been divided into three periods called French, Italian and English. This is not a true description, any more than that which would make of him a French poet merely, but it may be useful to bring out the importance of Chaucer's Italian studies. Chaucer was French in his literary education, to begin with, and in some respects he is French to the end. His verse is always French in pattern; he did not care for the English alliterative verse; he probably liked the English romance stanza better than he pretended, but he uses it only in the burlesque of *Sir Thopas*. In spite of his admiration for the Italian poets, he never imitates their verse, except in one short passage where he copies the *terza rima* of Dante. He is a great reader of Italian poems in the octave stanza, but he never uses that stanza; it was left for the Elizabethans. He translates a sonnet by Petrarch, but he does not follow the sonnet form. The strength and constancy of his devotion to French poetry is shown in the Prologue to the *Legend of Good Women*. The *Legend* was written just before the *Canterbury Tales*; that is to say, after what has been called the Italian period. But the ideas in the Prologue to the *Legend* are largely the ideas of the *Roman de la Rose*. As for the so-called English period, in which Chaucer is supposed to come to himself, to escape from his tutors, to deal immediately in his own way with the reality of English life, it is true that the *Canterbury Tales*, especially in the Prologue and the interludes and the comic stories, are full of observation and original and fresh descriptive work. But they are not better in this respect than *Troilus and Criseyde*, which is the chief thing in Chaucer's Italian period.

The importance of Chaucer's Italian reading is beyond doubt. But it does not displace the French masters in his affection. It adds something new to Chaucer's mind; it does not change his mind with regard to the things which he had learned to value in French poetry.

When it is said that an English period came to succeed the Italian in Chaucer's life, the real meaning of this is that Chaucer was all the time working for independence, and that, as he goes on, his original genius strengthens and he takes more and more of real life into his view. But there is no one period in which he casts off his foreign masters and strikes out absolutely for himself. Some of his greatest imaginative work, and the most original, is done in his adaptation of the story of Troilus from an Italian poem of Boccaccio.

Chaucer represents a number of common medieval tastes, and many of these had to be kept under control in his poetry. One can see him again and again tempted to indulge himself, and sometimes yielding, but generally securing his freedom and lifting his verse above the ordinary traditional ways. He has the educational bent very strongly. That is shown in his prose works. He is interested in popular philosophy and popular science; he translates 'Boece', the Consolation of Philosophy, and compiles the Treatise on the Astrolabe for 'little Lewis my son'. The tale of *Melibeus* which Chaucer

tells in his own person among the Canterbury pilgrims is a translation of a moral work which had an extraordinary reputation not
very easy to understand or appreciate now. Chaucer took it up no
doubt because it had been recommended by authors of good stand-
ing: he translates it from the French version by Jean de Meung.
The *Parson's Tale* is an adaptation from the French, and represents
the common form of good sermon literature. Chaucer thus shared
the tastes and the aptitudes of the good ordinary man of letters. He
was under no compulsion to do hack work; he wrote those things
because he was fond of studying and teaching, like the Clerk of
Oxford in the *Canterbury Tales*. The learning shown in his poems
is not pretence; it came into his poems because he had it in his mind.
How his wit could play with his science is shown in the *Hous of
Fame*, where the eagle is allowed to give a popular lecture on
acoustics, but is prevented from going on to astronomy. Chaucer dis-
sembles his interest in that subject because he knows that popular
science ought not to interfere too much with the proper business of
poetry; he also, being a humorist, sees the comic aspect of his own
didactic tastes; he sees the comic opposition between the teacher
anxious to go on explaining and the listener not so ready to take in
more. There is another passage, in *Troilus*, where good literary
advice is given (rather in the style of Polonius) against irrelevant
scientific illustrations. In a love-letter you must not allow your work
for the schools to appear too obviously—

> Ne jompre eek no discordant thing y-fere,
> As thus, to usen termes of physik.

This may be fairly interpreted as Chaucer talking to himself. He
knew that he was inclined to this sort of irrelevance and very apt to
drag in 'termes of physik', fragments of natural philosophy, where
they were out of place.

This was one of the things, one of the common medieval tempta-
tions, from which he had to escape if he was to be a master in the
art of poetry. How real the danger was can be seen in the works
of some of the Chaucerians, e.g. in Henryson's *Orpheus*, and in
Gawain Douglas's *Palace of Honour*.

Boethius is a teacher of a different sort from Melibeus, and the poet need not be afraid of him. Boethius, the master of Dante, the disciple of Plato, is one of the medieval authors who are not disqualified in any century; with him Chaucer does not require to be on his guard. The *Consolation of Philosophy* may help the poet even in the highest reach of his imagination; so Boethius is remembered by Chaucer, as he is by Dante, when he has to deal solemnly with the condition of men on earth. This is not one of the common medieval vanities from which Chaucer has to escape.

Far more dangerous and more attractive than any pedantry of the schools was the traditional convention of the allegorical poets, the *Rose* and all the attendants of the *Rose*. This was a danger that Chaucer could not avoid; indeed it was his chief poetical task, at first, to enter this dreamland and to come out of it with the spoils of the garden, which could not be won except by a dreamer and by full subjection to all the enchantments of the place. It was part of Chaucer's poetic vocation to comprehend and to make his own the whole spirit and language of the *Roman de la Rose* and also of the French poets who had followed, in the century between. The *Complaint to Pity* shows how he succeeded in this; also the *Complaint of Mars* and the poem called the *Complaint of Venus*, which is a translation from Oton de Granson, 'the floure of hem that maken in France'. Chaucer had to do this, and then he had to escape. This sort of fancy work, a kind of musical sentiment with a mythology of personified abstract qualities, is the least substantial of all things— thought and argument, imagery and utterance, all are of the finest and most impalpable.

> Thus am I slayn sith that Pité is deed:
> Allas the day! that ever hit shulde falle!
> What maner man dar now holde up his heed?
> To whom shall any sorwful herte calle,
> Now Crueltee hath cast to sleen us alle
> In ydel hope, folk redelees of peyne?
> Sith she is deed, to whom shul we compleyne

If this sort of verse had not been written, English poetry would have missed one of the graces of medieval art—a grace which at this day it is easy to despise. It is not despicable, but neither is it the

kind of beauty with which a strong imagination can be content, or
indeed any mind whatsoever, apart from such a tradition as that of
the old 'courtly makers'. And it is worth remembering that not
every one of the courtly makers restricted himself to this thin, fine
abstract melody. Eustache Deschamps, for example, amused himself with humorous verse as well; and for Froissart his ballades and
virelais were only a game, an occasional relief from the memoirs
in which he was telling the story of his time. Chaucer in fact did
very little in the French style of abstract sentiment. The longest of
his early poems, *The Book of the Duchess*, has much of this quality
in it, but this does not make the poem. *The Book of the Duchess*
is not abstract. It uses the traditional manner—dream, mythology,
and all— but it has other substance in it, and that is the character
of the Duchess Blanche herself, and the grief for her death. Chaucer
is here dealing with real life, and the conventional aids to poetry
are left behind.

How necessary it was to get beyond this French school is shown
by the later history of the French school itself. There was no one
like Chaucer in France; except perhaps Froissart, who certainly had
plenty of real life in his memoirs. But Froissart's Chronicles were
in prose, and did nothing to cure the inanition of French poetry,
which went on getting worse and worse, so that even a poetic genius
like Villon suffered from it, having no examples to guide him except
the thin ballades and rondeaux on the hackneyed themes. R. L.
Stevenson's account of Charles d'Orleans and his poetry will show
well enough what sort of work it was which was abandoned by
Chaucer, and which in the century after Chaucer was still the most
favoured kind in France.

It should not be forgotten that Chaucer, though he went far beyond such poetry as that of his French masters and of his own
Complaint to Pity, never turned against it. He escaped out of the
allegorical garden of the Rose, but with no resentment or ingrati-
tude. He never depreciates the old school. He must have criticized
it—to find it unsatisfying is to criticize it, implicitly at any rate; but
he never uses a word of blame or a sentence of parody. In his later
writings he takes up the devices of the Rose again; not only in the
Prologue to the *Legend of Good Women*, but also, though less obvi-

ously, in the *Squire's Tale*, where the sentiment is quite in harmony with the old French mode.

Chaucer wrote no such essay on poetry as Dante's *de Vulgari Eloquentia*; not even such a practical handbook of versification as was written by his friend Eustache Deschamps. But his writings, like Shakespeare's, have many passages referring to the literary art—the processes of the workshop—and a comparison of his poems with the originals which suggested them will often bring out what was consciously in his mind as he reflected on his work—as he calculated and altered, to suit the purpose which he had before him.

Chaucer is one of the greatest of literary artists, and one of the finest; so it is peculiarly interesting to make out what he thought of different poetical kinds and forms which came in his way through his reading or his own practice. For this object—i.e. to bring out Chaucer's aims and the way in which he criticized his own poetry—the most valuable evidence is given by the poem of *Anelida and the False Arcite*. This is not only an unfinished poem—Chaucer left many things unfinished—it is a poem which changes its purpose as it goes on, which is written under two different and discordant influences, and which could not possibly be made harmonious without total reconstruction from the beginning. It was written after Chaucer had gone some way in his reading of the Italian poets, and the opening part is copied from the *Teseide* of Boccaccio, which is also the original of the *Knight's Tale*. Now it was principally through Boccaccio's example that Chaucer learned how to break away from the French school. Yet here in this poem of *Anelida*, starting with imitation of Boccaccio, Chaucer goes back to the French manner, and works out a theme of the French school—and then drops it, in the middle of a sentence. He was distracted at that time, it is clear, between two opposite kinds of poetry. His *Anelida* is experimental work; in it we can see how he was changing his mind, and what difficulty he had with the new problems that were offered to him in his Italian books. He found in Italian a stronger kind of narrative than he had been accustomed to, outside of the Latin poets; a new kind of ambition, an attempt to rival the classical authors in a modern language. The *Teseide* (the *Theseid*) of Boccaccio is a modern epic poem in twelve books, meant by its author to be strong and solid and full; Chaucer in *Anelida* begins to translate and adapt this heroic poem—and then he turns away from the wars of Theseus to a story of disappointed love; further, he leaves the narrative style and composes for Anelida the most elaborate of all his lyric poems, the most extreme contrast to the heavy epic manner in which his poem is begun. The lyrical complaint of Anelida is the perfection of everything that had been tried in the French school—a fine unsubstantial beauty so thin and clear that it is hardly comprehensible at first, and never in agreement with the forcible narrative verse at the beginning of the poem.

Chaucer here has been caught escaping from the Garden of the Rose; he has heard outside the stronger music of the new Italian epic poetry, but the old devotion is for the time too strong, and he falls back. His return is not exactly failure, because the complaint of Anelida, which is in many respects old-fashioned, a kind of poetry very near exhaustion, is also one of the most elaborate things ever composed by Chaucer, such a proof of his skill in verse as he never gives elsewhere.

The *Teseide* kept him from sleeping, and his later progress cannot be understood apart from this epic of Boccaccio. When Chaucer read the Italian poets, he found them working with a new conception of the art of poetry, and particulary a fresh comprehension of the Ancients. The classical Renaissance has begun.

The influence of the Latin poets had been strong all through the Middle Ages. In its lowest degree it helped the medieval poets to find matter for their stories; the French *Roman d'Eneas* is the work that shows this best, because it is a version of the greatest Latin poem, and can be easily compared with its original, so as to find out what is understood and what is missed or travestied; how far the scope of the *Aeneid* is different from the old French order of romance.

But neither here nor generally elsewhere is the debt limited to the matter of stories. The sentiment, the pathos, the eloquence of medieval French poetry is derived from Virgil and Ovid. The Latin poets are the originals of medieval romance, far beyond what can be reckoned by any comparison of plots and incidents. And the medieval poets in their turn are the ancestors of the Renaissance and show the way to modern poetry.

But the old French poets, though they did much for the classical education of Europe, were inattentive to many things in classical poetry which the Italians were the first to understand, even before the revival of Greek, and which they appropriated for modern verse in time for Chaucer to be interested in what they were doing. Shortly, they understood what was meant by composition, proportion, the narrative unities; they appreciated the style of Latin poetry as the French did not; in poetical ornament they learned from Virgil something more spiritual and more imaginative than the French had known, and for which the term 'ornament' is hardly good enough; it is found in the similes of Dante, and after him in Chaucer.

This is one of the most difficult and one of the most interesting parts of literary history—the culmination and the end of the Middle Ages, in which the principles of medieval poetry are partly justified and partly refuted. As seen in the work of Chaucer, the effect of this new age and the Italian poetry was partly the stronger and richer poetical language and (an obvious sign of this strengthening) the similes such as were used by the classical authors. But far more than this, a change was made in the whole manner of devising and shaping a story. This change was suggested by the Italian poets; it fell in with the change in Chaucer's own mind and with the independent growth of his strength. What he learned as a critic from study he used as an artist at the time when his imaginative power was quickest and most fertile. Yet before his journey to Italy, and apparently before he had learnt any Italian, he had already gone some way to meet the new poetry, without knowing it.

His earlier narrative poems, afterwards used for the tales of the Second Nun, the Clerk of Oxford and the Man of Law, have at least one quality in which they agree both with the Italians and with Chaucer's maturest work. The verse is stately, strong, *heroic* in more senses than one. Chaucer's employment of the ten-syllable line in the seven-line stanza for narrative was his own discovery. The decasyllabic line was an old measure; so was the seven-line stanza, both in Provençal and French. But the stanza had been generally restricted to lyric poetry, as in Chaucer's *Complaint to Pity*. It was a favourite stanza for ballades. French poetry discouraged the stanza in narrative verse; the common form for narrative of all sorts, and for preaching and satire as well, was the short couplet—the verse of the *Roman de Troie,* the *Roman de Renart,* the *Roman de la Rose*, the verse of the *Book of the Duchess* and the *Hous of Fame*. When Chaucer used the longer verse in his *Life of St. Cecilia* and the other earlier tales, it is probable that he was following a common English opinion and taste, which tended against the universal dominion of the short couplet. 'Short verse' was never put out of use or favour, never insulted or condemned. But the English seem to have felt that it was not enough; they wanted more varieties. They had the alliterative verse, and, again, the use of the *rime couée*—*Sir Thopas* verse—was certainly due to a wish for variety. The long verse of Robert of Gloucester was another possibility, frequently taken. After Chaucer's time, and seemingly independent of him, there were, in the fifteenth century, still more varieties in use amongst the minstrels. There was a general feeling among poets of all degrees that the short couplet (with no disrespect to it) was not the only and was not the most powerful of instruments. The technical originality of Chaucer was, first, that he learned the secret of the ten-syllable line, and later that he used it for regular narrative and made it the proper heroic verse in English. The most remarkable thing in this discovery is that Chaucer began to conform to the Italian rule before he knew anything about it. Not only are his single lines much nearer to the Italian rhythm than the French. This is curious, but it is not exceptional; it is what happens generally when the French decasyllable is imitated in one of the Teutonic languages, and Gower, who knew no Italian, or at any rate shows no sign of attending to Italian poetry, writes his occasional decasyllabic lines in the same way as Chaucer. But besides this mode of the single verse Chaucer agrees with the Italian practice in using stanzas for long narrative poetry; here he seems to have been led instinctively, or at least without any conscious imitation, to agree with the poet whom he was to follow still further, when once Boccaccio came in sight. This coincidence of taste in metre was one thing that must have struck Chaucer as soon as he opened an Italian

book. Dante and Boccaccio used the same type of line as Chaucer
had taken for many poems before ever he learned Italian; while the
octave stanzas of Boccaccio's epic—the common verse, before that,
of the Italian minstrels in their romances—must have seemed to
Chaucer remarkably like his own stanza in the *Life of St. Cecilia*
or the story of *Constance*.

This explains how it was that Chaucer, with all his admiration
for Italian poetry, never, except in one small instance, tries to copy
any Italian verse. He did not copy the Italian line because he had
the same line already from another source; and he did not copy
Boccaccio's octave stanza because he had already another stanza
quite as good, if not better, in the same kind. One need not consider
long, what is also very probable, that Chaucer felt the danger
of too great attraction to those wonderful new models; he would
learn what he could (so he seems to have thought to himself), but
he would not give up what he had already gained without them.
Possibly the odd change of key, the relapse from Italian to French
style in *Anelida*, might be explained as Chaucer's reaction against
the too overpowering influence of the new Italian school. 'Here is
this brand-new epic starting out to conquer all the world; no
question but that it is triumphant, glorious, successful; and we cannot escape; but before we join in the procession, and it is too late
to draw back, suppose we draw back *now*—into the old garden—
to try once more what may be made of the old French kind of
music.' So possibly we might translate into ruder terms what seems
to be the artistic movement in this remarkable failure by Chaucer.

Chaucer spent a long time thinking over the Italian poetry which
he had learned, and he made different attempts to turn it to profit
in English before he succeeded. One of his first complete poems after
his Italian studies had begun is as significant as *Anelida* both with
respect to the difficulties that he found and also to the enduring
influence of the French school. In the *Parliament of Birds*, his style
as far as it can be tested in single passages seems to have learned
everything there was to be learned—

> Through me men goon into the blisful place
> Of hertès hele and dedly woundès cure;

> Through me men goon unto the welle of Grace
> There grene and lusty May shal ever endure;
> This is the way to all good aventure;
> Be glad, thou reader, and thy sorrow offcaste!
> All open am I; passe in and hy thee faste!

And, as for composition, the poem carries out to the full what the author intends; the digressions and the slackness that are felt to detract from the *Book of the Duchess* have been avoided; the poem expresses the mind of Chaucer, both through the music of its solemn verse, and through the comic dialogue of the birds in their assembly. But this accomplished piece of work, with all its reminiscences of Dante and Boccaccio, is old French in its scheme; it is another of the allegorical dreams, and the device of the Parliament of Birds is in French older than the *Romaunt of the Rose*.

Chaucer is still, apparently, holding back; practising on the ground familiar to him, and gradually working into his poetry all that he can readily manage out of his Italian books. In *Anelida* Italian and French are separate and discordant; in the *Parliament of Birds* there is a harmony, but as yet Chaucer has not matched himself thoroughly against Boccaccio. When he does so, in *Troilus* and in the *Knight's Tale*, it will be found that he is something more than a translator, and more than an adapter of minor and separable passages.

The *Teseide* of Boccaccio is at last after many attempts—how many, it is impossible to say—rendered into English by Chaucer, not in a translation, but with a thorough recasting of the whole story. *Troilus and Criseyde* is taken from another poem by Boccaccio. *Troilus* and the *Knight's Tale* are without rivals in English for the critical keenness which has gone into them. Shakespeare has the same skill in dealing with his materials, in choosing and rejecting, but Shakespeare was never matched, as Chaucer was in these works, against an author of his own class, an author, too, who had all the advantages of long training. The interest—the historical interest at any rate—of Chaucer's dealings with Boccaccio is that it was an encounter between an Englishman whose education had been chiefly French, and an Italian who had begun upon the ways of the new learning. To put it bluntly, it was the Middle Ages against the

Renaissance; and the Englishman won on the Italian ground and under the Italian rules. Chaucer judged more truly than Boccaccio what the story of Palamon and Arcite was worth; the story of Troilus took shape in his imagination with incomparably more strength and substance. In both cases he takes what he thinks fit; he learned from Boccaccio, or perhaps it would be truer to say he found out for himself in reading Boccaccio what was the value of right proportion in narrative. He refused altogether to be led away as Boccaccio was by the formal classical ideal of epic poetry—the 'receipt to make an epic poem' which prescribed as necessary all the things employed in the construction of the *Aeneid*. Boccaccio is the first modern author who writes an epic in twelve books; and one of his books is taken up with funeral games, because Virgil in the *Aeneid* had imitated the funeral games in Homer. In the time of Pope this was still a respectable tradition. Chaucer is not tempted; he keeps to what is essential, and in the proportions of his story and his conception of the narrative unities he is saner than all the Renaissance.

One of the finest passages in English criticism of poetry is Dryden's estimate of Chaucer in the Preface to the *Fables*. Chaucer is taken by Dryden, in the year 1700, as an example of that sincerity and truth to Nature which makes the essence of classical poetry. In this classical quality, Dryden thinks that Ovid is far inferior to Chaucer. Dryden makes allowance for Chaucer's old-fashioned language, and he did not fully understand the beauty of Chaucer's verse, but still he judges him as a modern writer with respect to his imagination; to no modern writer does he give higher praise than to Chaucer.

This truth to Nature, in virtue of which Chaucer is a classic, will be found to be limited in some of his works by conventions which are not always easy to understand. Among these should not be reckoned the dream allegory. For though it may appear strange at first that Chaucer should have gone back to this in so late a work as the Prologue to the *Legend of Good Women*, yet it does not prevent him from speaking his mind either in earlier or later poems. In the *Book of the Duchess*, the *Parliament of Birds*, the Prologue to the *Legend*, one feels that Chaucer is dealing with life, and saying what he really thinks, in spite of the conventions. The *Hous of Fame*, which is a

dream poem, might almost have been written for a wager, to show
that he could bring in everything traditional, everything most
common in the old artificial poetry, and yet be original and fresh
through it all. But there are some stories—the *Clerk's Tale*, and the
Franklin's Tale—in which he uses conventions of another sort and is
partially disabled by them. These are stories of a kind much favoured
in the Middle Ages, turning each upon one single obligation which,
for the time, is regarded as if it were the only rule of conduct. The
patience of Griselda is absolute; nothing must be allowed to interfere with it, and there is no other moral in the story. It is one of the
frequent medieval examples in which the author can only think of
one thing at a time. On working out this theme, Chaucer is really
tried as severely as his heroine, and his patience is more extraordinary,
because if there is anything certain about him it is that his mind
is never satisfied with any one single aspect of any matter. Yet here
he carries the story through to the end, though when it is finished
he writes an epilogue which is a criticism on the strained morality
of the piece. The plot of the *Franklin's Tale* is another of the
favourite medieval type, where the 'point of honour', the obligation
of a vow, is treated in the same uncompromising way; Chaucer is
here confined to a problem under strict rules, a drama of difficulties
without character.

In the *Legend of Good Women* he is limited in a different way,
and not so severely. He has to tell 'the Saints' Lives of Cupid'—the
Legends of the Heroines who have been martyrs for love; and as
in the Legend of the Saints of the Church, the same motives are
repeated, the trials of loyalty, the grief and pity. The Legend was
left unfinished, apparently because Chaucer was tired. Yet it is not
certain that he repented of his plan, or that the plan was wrong.
There may possibly have been in this work something of the formal-
ism which is common in Renaissance art, the ambition to build up
a structure in many compartments, each compartment resembling
all the others in the character of the subject and its general lines.
But the stories are distinct, and all are beautiful—the legends of
Cleopatra Queen and Martyr, of Thisbe and Ariadne, and the rest.
Another poem which may be compared with the *Legend of Good
Women* is the *Monk's Tale*—an early work to which Chaucer

made later additions—his book of the *Falls of Princes*. The Canterbury pilgrims find it too depressing, and in their criticism of the Monk's tragedies Chaucer may possibly have been thinking also of his unfinished *Legend of Good Women*. But what has been said of the Legend may be repeated about the *Monk's Tale*; there is the same kind of pathos in all the chapters, but they are all varied. One of the tragedies is the most considerable thing which Chaucer took from Dante; the story of Ugolino in the *Inferno*, 'Hugelyn Erle of Pise'.

It is uncertain whether Chaucer knew the *Decameron* of Boccaccio, but the art of his comic stories is very like that of the Italian, to whom he owed so much in other ways. It is the art of comic imagination, using a perfect style which does not need to be compared with the unsophisticated old French ribaldry of the *fabliaux* to be appreciated, though a comparison of that sort will show how far the Middle Ages had been left behind by Boccaccio and Chaucer. Among the interludes in the *Canterbury Tales* there are two especially, the monologues of the Wife of Bath and the Pardoner, where Chaucer has discovered one of the most successful forms of comic poetry, and the Canon's Yeoman's prologue may be reckoned as a third along with them, though there, and also in the *Canon's Yeoman's Tale*, the humour is of a peculiar sort, with less character in it, and more satire—like the curious learned satire of which Ben Jonson was fond. It is remarkable that the tales told by the Wife of Bath and the Pardoner are both in a different tone from their discourses about themselves.

Without *Troilus and Criseyde* the works of Chaucer would be an immense variety—romance and sentiment, humour and observation, expressed in poetical language that has never been equalled for truth and liveliness. But it is only in *Troilus* that Chaucer uses his full powers together in harmony. All the world, it might be said, is reflected in the various poems of Chaucer; *Troilus* is the one poem which brings it all into a single picture. In the history of English poetry it is the close of the Middle Ages.

Bibliographical Notes
by Pamela Gradon

THESE BIBLIOGRAPHICAL NOTES are designed to replace both W. P. Ker's original Note on Books and R. W. Chambers's supplementary note written in 1942. It is hoped that a selective bibliography of this kind will be in keeping with Ker's refusal to add an elaborate bibliography to his book.

I. GRAMMARS, DICTIONARIES, AND READERS

The beginner may supplement H. Sweet's *Anglo-Saxon Primer*, revised by N. Davis (9th edn., Oxford and New York, 1953) by R. Quirk and C. L. Wrenn, *An Old English Grammar* (revised, London, 1958). The Old English grammar for advanced students is A. Campbell, *Old English Grammar* (Oxford, 1959). Sweet's *Student's Dictionary of Anglo-Saxon* (Oxford and New York, 1897) and J. R. Clark Hall's *Concise Anglo-Saxon Dictionary* (4th edn. with suppl., Cambridge, 1960) are useful companions to texts, although the student may need to consult J. Bosworth and T. N. Toller, *An Anglo-Saxon Dictionary* and *Supplement* (Oxford and New York, 1898, 1921) for more abstruse points. Sweet's *Anglo-Saxon Reader*, an indispensable collection of texts for the student, has now been revised by D. Whitelock (15th edn., Oxford and New York, 1967).

For the later period a useful collection of texts is provided by J. A. W. Bennett, G. V. Smithers, and N. Davis, *Early Middle English Verse and Prose* (Oxford and New York, 1966) and K. Sisam, *Fourteenth Century Verse and Prose* (Oxford and New York, 1921). There is no satisfactory text-book dealing with the language of this period, but some information may be obtained from G. K. W. Johnston's translation of Brunner, *An Outline of Middle English Grammar* (Cambridge, Mass., 1963); F. Mossé, translated by J. A. Walker, *A Handbook of Middle English* (Baltimore, 1952); or S. Moore and A. H. Marckwardt, *Historical Outlines of English Sounds and Inflections* (Ann Arbor, 1951). Indispensable tools for the study of the language are *The Oxford English Dictionary* and, for more advanced students, the *Middle English Dictionary* edited by H. Kurath, S. M. Kuhn, and J. Reidy (Ann Arbor, 1954 ff.). For Middle English syntax consult T. F. Mustanoja, *A Middle English Syntax*, Part I (Helsinki, 1960).

2. BIBLIOGRAPHIES

It would be impossible to review editions of, or monographs on, all the poems or authors mentioned in this book; nor would it be possible to catalogue the vast body of material in periodicals. For extensive information the student must consult bibliographies such as *The Cambridge Bibliography of English Language and Literature* and *Supplement* edited by F. W. Bateson (Cambridge, 1940, 1957); or the exhaustive and more authoritative work of J. E. Wells, *A Manual of the Writings in Middle English, 1050–1400* and *Supplements* (New Haven, 1916–51). The first volume of a revised reprint edited by J. Burke Severs has now appeared and has been extended to include the fifteenth century (New Haven, 1967). For Chaucer the following may be consulted: E. P. Hammond, *Chaucer: A Bibliographical Manual* (New York, 1933); D. D. Griffith, *Bibliography of Chaucer, 1908–1953* (Seattle, 1955); W. R. Crawford, *Bibliography of Chaucer* (Seattle, 1967). For the Old English period the student may use, not only the *Cambridge Bibliography*, but also A. H. Heusinkveld and E. J. Bashe, *A Bibliographical Guide to Old English* (Iowa Humanistic Studies, iv, 5: Iowa City, 1931). The periodical bibliographies, *The Year's Work in English Studies* and *The Annual Bibliography of English Language and Literature*, published by the Modern Humanities Research Association, are also useful.

3. TEXTS

Nevertheless, some texts or collections of texts may be noted, especially those which fall outside the chronological limits of standard bibliographies. F. Klaeber's edition of *Beowulf*, still the best, now exists in a third edition (reprinted with second supplement, London, 1950; Boston, 1951), and R. W. Chambers, *Beowulf, an Introduction* is available also in a third edition revised by C. L. Wrenn (Cambridge, 1959). This includes a very full bibliography. Apart from *Beowulf*, interest in this period has centred chiefly in the elegies, of which there have been three recent editions all containing useful bibliography: I. L. Gordon, *The Seafarer* (London and New York, 1960); R. F. Leslie, *Three Old English Elegies* (Manchester and New York, 1961); and R. F. Leslie, *The Wanderer* (Manchester and New York, 1966). The *Andreas* has recently been edited by K. R. Brooks (Oxford and New York, 1961) and the *Phoenix* by N. F. Blake (Manchester and New York, 1964). For the prose D. Bethurum's *The Homilies of Wulfstan* (Oxford and New York, 1957) may be noted, and J. C. Pope's *Homilies of Aelfric: A Supplementary Collection* (Early English Text Society, Orig. Ser. 259, 260, 1967, 1968). *The Anglo-Saxon Poetic Records*, edited by G. P. Krapp and E. V. K. Dobbie (New York, 1931–53) provide a corpus of Anglo-Saxon poetry, although the lack of a glossary limits its usefulness for beginners. For the Middle English period we may note a number of useful collections of texts and some convenient modern series. For the lyrics we have the collections of Carleton Brown: *English Lyrics of the XIIIth Century, Religious Lyrics of the XIVth Century* (revised by G. V. Smithers), and *Religious Lyrics of the XVth Century* (Oxford and New York, 1932, 1952, 1939); and of R. H. Robbins: *Secular Lyrics of the XIVth and XVth Centuries* (Oxford and New York, 1952), and *Historical Poems of the XIV and XVth Centuries* (New York,

1959). A useful collection of lyrics, with normalized spelling and a good introduction, is R. T. Davies, *Medieval English Lyrics* (London and Evanston, Ill.,
1963). The collection of romances by W. H. French and C. B. Hale, *Middle
English Metrical Romances* (New York, 1930) is available in a reprint and F. J.
Child's standard work, *English and Scottish Popular Ballads* (Oxford, reprinted
1965) is also available in a paperback edition (New York, 1965). For devotional
prose E. Colledge, *The Medieval Mystics of England* (London and New York,
1962) may be recommended. The Nelson Medieval and Renaissance Library
contains some useful volumes such as *The Ancrene Wisse*, Parts VI and VII,
edited by G. Shepherd (London and Edinburgh, and New York, 1959); *The
Owl and the Nightingale*, edited by E. G. Stanley (1960); and Thomas Chestre's
Sir Launfal, edited by A. J. Bliss (1960), which makes a companion volume to
his edition of *Sir Orfeo* (2nd edn., Oxford and New York, 1966). A convenient
introduction to some of the lengthier fifteenth- and early sixteenth-century
authors is provided by the Clarendon Medieval and Tudor Series: *John Lydgate:
Poems* edited by J. Norton-Smith (Oxford and New York, 1966); D. F. C. Cold-
well's *Selections from Gavin Douglas* (1964); *William Dunbar* by J. Kinsley
(1958); *Robert Henryson* by C. Elliott (1963); and R. L. Greene's *A Selection of
English Carols* (1962), a partial replacement of the now unobtainable *Early
English Carols* (Oxford, 1935); *The Paston Letters*, edited N. Davis (1958).

Ever since Chambers wrote his bibliographical note in 1942 there has been
much advance in the publication and study of texts. The monumental *Text of
the 'Canterbury Tales'* by J. M. Manly and E. Rickert (Chicago, 1940) is a
landmark in Chaucer studies, although only suitable for the advanced student.
More relevant for the average reader of Chaucer is the second edition of F. N.
Robinson's *Works of Geoffrey Chaucer* (Oxford and New York, 1957). Progress
has also been made in the study of the texts of *Piers Plowman*: of the A-text in
A Critical Edition of the A-Version by T. A. Knott and D. C. Fowler (Baltimore,
1952), and *'Piers Plowman': the A-version* by G. Kane (London and New York,
1960); and of the C-text in *The C-Text and its Poet* by E. T. Donaldson (New
Haven, 1949). For Malory there is a new revised edition of E. Vinaver's *Works
of Sir Thomas Malory* (Oxford and New York, 1967). The revised edition, by
N. Davis, of Tolkien and Gordon's *Sir Gawain and the Green Knight* (2nd edn.,
Oxford, 1968) is published in paperback as well as cloth. W. W. Skeat's edition
of *The Lay of Havelok the Dane* was revised by K. Sisam (2nd edn., Oxford and
New York, 1915). There are also the many texts published by the Early English
Text Society, some of which reflect areas of interest new since Ker wrote, such
as the devotional writings represented by *The Cloud of Unknowing* edited by
P. Hodgson (EETS, O.S. 218, 1944); *The Book of Margery Kempe*, edited by
S. B. Meech and H. E. Allen (EETS, O.S. 212, 1940); and *The Ancrene Wisse*,
edited by J. R. R. Tolkien (EETS, O.S. 249, 1962). The latter has been translated
by M. Salu, *The Ancrene Riwle* (London and Notre Dame, 1955).

4. CRITICAL STUDIES

The vitality of medieval studies since World War II is evident in the abundance
of critical studies and in the development of new areas of interest. In the Old
English period the most notable has been the interest in the 'formulaic style'
(cp. A. B. Lord, *The Singer of Tales* (Cambridge, Mass., 1960)), but more tradi-

tional studies are represented by D. Whitelock, *The Audience of 'Beowulf'* (Oxford and New York, 1951); A. C. Brodeur, *The Art of 'Beowulf'* (Berkeley, 1959); and E. B. Irving, *A Reading of 'Beowulf'* (New Haven, 1968). A valuable collection of studies of the main Old English monuments, with full bibliography, is *Continuations and Beginnings* edited by E. G. Stanley (London and Edinburgh, 1966). L. E. Nicholson has made *An Anthology of 'Beowulf' Criticism* (Notre Dame, 1963) which includes articles of various dates and critical standpoints. In Middle English, critical interest has been made diffused. Of the abundant works on Chaucer the following are especially useful: J. A. W. Bennett, *The Parlement of Foules* (Oxford and New York, 1957) and *Chaucer's Book of Fame* (Oxford, 1968); S. B. Meech, *Design in Chaucer's 'Troilus'* (Syracuse, N.Y., 1959); C. Muscatine, *Chaucer and the French Tradition* (Berkeley, 1957); and J. S. P. Tatlock, *The Mind and Art of Chaucer* (Syracuse, N.Y., 1950). Collections of critical essays have been made by E. Wagenknecht in *Chaucer: Modern Essays in Criticism* (New York, 1959); and R. J. Schoeck and J. Taylor in *Chaucer Criticism* (Notre Dame, 1960–1). For Langland the most useful introduction to the criticism of the text is perhaps still T. P. Dunning, *'Piers Plowman': an Interpretation of the A-Text* (Dublin, 1937), but the following more recent books are also helpful: J. Lawlor, *'Piers Plowman': An Essay in Criticism* (London and New York, 1962); and R. W. Frank, *'Piers Plowman' and the Scheme of Salvation* (New Haven, 1957). J. H. Fisher has written a much needed book on Gower: *John Gower: Moral Philosopher and Friend of Chaucer* (New York, 1964). The standard introduction to the ballads is M. J. C. Hodgart, *The Ballads* (London, 1950, paperback New York, 1966), G. H. Gerould, *The Ballad of Tradition* (London, 1932; New York, 1957) is useful. Little work has appeared on sermons since G. R. Owst published *Preaching in Medieval England* (Cambridge, 1926; New York, 1965), but *Literature and Pulpit in Medieval England* now exists in a second edition (Oxford and New York, 1961). For the drama there is a good introduction in H. Craig, *English Religious Drama* (Oxford and New York, 1955), and an admirable study of staging in G. Wickham, *Early English Stages, 1300–1600*, Vol. I (London and New York, 1959). Something of the range of critical interest aroused by medieval literature appears in the recent studies of *Sir Gawain and the Green Knight* and *Pearl*: *A Reading of 'Sir Gawain and the Green Knight'* by J. A. Burrow (London, 1965; New York, 1966); *Art and Tradition in 'Sir Gawain and the Green Knight'* by L. D. Benson (New Brunswick, N.J., 1965); and *The 'Pearl': An Interpretation* by P. M. Kean (London and New York, 1967). Critical essays have been collected by R. J. Blanch in *'Sir Gawain' and 'Pearl': Critical Essays* (Bloomington, 1966). For alliterative poetry generally the best study is probably D. Everett, *Essays on Middle English Literature* (Oxford and New York, 1955). Vinaver's discovery of the Winchester Manuscript of the *Morte D'Arthur* gave a new impetus to Malory studies. A survey is usefully provided by the collection of essays, with bibliography, edited by J. A. W. Bennett, *Essays on Malory* (Oxford and New York, 1963). A rather different approach is represented by R. M. Lumiansky, *Malory's Originality* (Baltimore, 1964). For Arthurian material the best reference book is R. S. Loomis, *Arthurian Literature in the Middle Ages* (Oxford, 1959). Literary history is to be found in the following volumes of the Oxford History of English Literature: E. K. Chambers, *English Literature at the Close of the Middle Ages* (1947); H. S. Bennett, *Chaucer and the Fifteenth Century* (1948);

C. S. Lewis, *English Literature in the Sixteenth Century* (1954), which deals with late medieval poetry. Background studies, too, have been productive. The kind of comparative study favoured by W. P. Ker had a notable successor in C. S. Lewis's *Allegory of Love* (Oxford and New York, 1936); more recently, the association between literature, art, and devotional practice, interest in which was widely fostered by Emile Mâle's *The Gothic Image* (New York, 1958; London, 1961), has been the subject of a study by R. Woolf in *The Middle English Lyric* (Oxford, 1968). Study of the patristic background to medieval literature has given rise to much critical discussion. An extreme and very controversial document here is D. W. Robertson's *Preface to Chaucer* (Princeton, 1963). The Latin background of medieval literature is dealt with by C. S. Lewis in *The Discarded Image* (Cambridge, 1964). E. R. Curtius, *European Literature and the Latin Middle Ages* (a translation by W. R. Trask, London and Princeton, 1953) and E. Auerbach, *Mimesis* (a translation by W. R. Trask, Princeton, 1953) are works which have given a new slant to the criticism of medieval literature.

5. BACKGROUND STUDIES

Readers acquainted with W. P. Ker's other works, such as *Epic and Romance* and *The Dark Ages*, will realize how fundamental to his thinking about medieval literature were the concepts 'heroic' and 'courtly'. It would seem fitting, therefore, to conclude with some indication of reading in these fields. Ker's own *Epic and Romance* (2nd edn., London and New York, 1908) is still perhaps the best introduction to the 'heroic' in Germanic and medieval literature. A useful recent book is B. J. Timmer's translation of J. de Vries, *Heroic Song and Heroic Legend* (Oxford and New York, 1963). For the courtly and chivalric background consult E. Prestage, *Chivalry* (London, 1928); S. Painter, *French Chivalry* (Baltimore, 1940); M. Bloch, *Feudal Society* (a translation by L. A. Manyon, 2 vols., 2nd edn., Chicago, 1961; London, 1962). A reading of the numerous translations of Icelandic sagas and of French works such as *The Romance of the Rose*, should help readers to grasp the literary implications of the terms 'heroic' and 'courtly'.

1968

Index